In times of crisis, leadership th [...] inspires growth, and creates a resilience culture that radiates to all aspects of life is priceless. This book inspires the growth of such leadership like none other I've read. It masterfully integrates leadership, crisis management, and resilience—brilliantly weaving together research, application, inspiration, and wisdom. Heroic leadership is not simple, or easy, but this work makes it as simple and achievable as possible. It will help any leader or aspiring leader. If you read only one leadership book, this could be the one. I'll refer to it again and again. I enthusiastically recommend it.

—**GLENN R. SCHIRALDI, PHD, LT. COL. (USAR, RET.),** UNIVERSITY OF MARYLAND SCHOOL OF PUBLIC HEALTH (RET.), COLLEGE PARK, MD, UNITED STATES; AUTHOR, *WORLD WAR II SURVIVORS: LESSONS IN RESILIENCE*; *THE RESILIENCE WORKBOOK*; *THE ADVERSE CHILDHOOD EXPERIENCES RECOVERY WORKBOOK*

As if to reinforce the adage "necessity is the mother of invention," one of the pioneers in his field, Dr. Everly links three crucial topics of our time (effective leadership, resilience, and crisis management) in a practical, easy-to-read book that should be studied by all who have been tasked to keep us safe and prospering. For their sake and ours, I hope *Leading Beyond Crisis* will set the new standard for how our leaders, no matter what their domain, are measured.

—**ALAN M. LANGLIEB, MD, MPH, MBA,** COEDITOR, *MENTAL HEALTH AND PRODUCTIVITY IN THE WORKPLACE*; MEDICAL DIRECTOR, INPATIENT PSYCHIATRY, MEDSTAR GEORGETOWN UNIVERSITY HOSPITAL; ASSOCIATE PROFESSOR, GEORGETOWN UNIVERSITY SCHOOL OF MEDICINE, WASHINGTON, DC, UNITED STATES

Leading Beyond Crisis: The Five Pillars of Transformative Resilient Leadership is a masterful guide to that rare ability to lead through and beyond crisis, building stronger people and organizations along the way. The ability to develop a culture of resilience has never been more essential to the people and organizations that leaders serve. Everly and Athey teach us how to lead in the most effective of ways. This book is essential reading for all interested in leadership. Prepare to be inspired to lead in a strong, bold, and honorable way. This is a transformative read!

—VICTOR WELZANT, PSYD, INTERNATIONAL CRITICAL INCIDENT STRESS FOUNDATION, INC., ELLICOTT CITY, MD, UNITED STATES

LEADING
BEYOND
CRISIS

LEADING
BEYOND
CRISIS

· ·

THE FIVE PILLARS OF
TRANSFORMATIVE
RESILIENT LEADERSHIP

· ·

GEORGE S. EVERLY, JR.
PHD, ABPP, FACLP, FAPA

AMY B. ATHEY
PSYD, CMPC

 AMERICAN PSYCHOLOGICAL ASSOCIATION

The opinions and statements published are the responsibility of the authors, and such opinions and statements do not necessarily represent the policies of the American Psychological Association.

Published by
APA LifeTools
750 First Street, NE
Washington, DC 20002
https://www.apa.org

Order Department
https://www.apa.org/pubs/books
order@apa.org

In the U.K., Europe, Africa, and the Middle East, copies may be ordered from Eurospan
https://www.eurospanbookstore.com/apa
info@eurospangroup.com

Typeset in Sabon by Circle Graphics, Inc., Reisterstown, MD

Printer: Gasch Printing, Odenton, MD
Cover Designer: Mark Karis

Library of Congress Cataloging-in-Publication Data

CIP data has been applied for. Library of Congress Control Number: 2022946736

https://doi.org/10.1037/0000323-000

Printed in the United States of America

10 9 8 7 6 5 4 3 2 1

CONTENTS

LEADING
BEYOND
CRISIS

TRANSFORMATIVE RESILIENT LEADERSHIP DEFINED

Leadership in the best of times is challenging. Leadership in crisis is harder still. But there is a third type of leadership that must certainly be the most challenging of all—one that seizes upon adversity and even crisis as an opportunity for transformation and growth. Imagine a leader who can practice transformative leadership anchored in growth-promoting resilience that propels people, organizations, and even communities to greater heights than before, greater heights than perhaps imagined. Imagine the leader who can not only lead to bounce back but foster quantum leaps forward from the abyss of crisis is a rare person, indeed. "The moment [such a leader] takes the helm, order, promptitude and confidence follow as the necessary result. When we see such results, we know that a hero leads" (Wanted a leader, 1861, p. 4).

Leadership is the ability to influence or guide others. It is the force that harnesses and shapes social energy into a social force. *Transformative resilient leadership* is our term to describe those crisis leadership behaviors that foster organizational, community, and personal growth in the wake of adversity. It guides through the "fog of crisis" with the promise of a better future. The Institute of Medicine (IOM) of the National Academies (IOM, 2013) wrote that highly effective leaders can increase resilience to stressful conditions and may even lead to the creation of an entire culture of resilience that radiates to all aspects of the organization, and perhaps the community, as well. We believe that with the right leadership, crisis can create a "tipping point" that leads to such change. Transformative crisis leadership combines guidance and spirit to not only heal but also evolve the culture forward with the strength of resilience and growth.

There are books on leadership. There are books on crisis. There are books on resilience. This book uses research on all three topics to present a model of transformative resilient leadership. Transformative resilient leadership includes five prominent *pillars*, or characteristics. These pillars are found in the "classics" of modern leadership theory as well as in our own research. Transformative resilient leaders possess and deploy

- a clear *vision*, which mitigates the negative impact of the crisis at hand and leverages the community, organizational, and individual strengths to grow;
- *decisiveness* in their decision-making processes;
- *effective communication* that conveys this vision and direction to empower the collective for growth;
- *supportive relationships* to not only withstand individual and collective stress but act as a catalyst for growth; and
- *integrity* that underlies all leadership actions.

This book is written by a teacher (Dr. Everly) and his former student (Dr. Athey), who reconnected 20 years after their initial introduction to build an innovative resilience-based program for a large state university. Yes, the pandemic can bring about connection. Written from this unique combination of perspectives, our team taps the expertise of a public health scholar and disaster psychologist (Dr. Everly) whose 48-year career has involved travel to 39 countries on six continents and consisted of cofounding and codirecting for-profit health care organizations as well as a United Nations-affiliated nonprofit organization. Additionally, we have the experience of a former collegiate All-American basketball player (Dr. Athey) who went on to become a national leading sport and performance psychologist, a high-ranking university administrator, and a performance psychologist for elite special warfare operators.

Over the past 4 decades, we have each researched and written about the signs indicating that an organization or group possesses an organizational culture of resilience. Shared aspirations and goals that are clearly defined and easily measured are essential for the collective group. Resilient organizations demonstrate reciprocal support and collaboration among members. Think of it as a Three Musketeers "one for all and all for one" approach. There is also an attitude of "no one left behind" in a crisis. There is a collaborative interdependency, wherein the success of the individual is intertwined with the overall success of the organization, and success is maximized through collaboration. Additionally, the members of the organization possess shared values in terms of how the organization's goals should be achieved, and there exists a high degree of cohesion. *Cohesion* is the degree to which there exists a social affinity of members for other members and leadership. There is an esprit de corps characterized by mutual respect and trust among members and between members and leadership. Last, group members identify with the organization's "brand." There is pride associated with membership. Members may even derive some degree of their personal identity from their membership in the group.

Yet, although many group leaders know these factors matter for organizational resilience, they often do not know how to facilitate such transformation. Given this, we have created a prescriptive approach to the practice of transformative resilient leadership.

DEVELOPING OUR PRESCRIPTIVE APPROACH

Based on work originally done in China, we coauthored a book on resilient leadership in 2010. For the most part, it was a prescriptive book on the leadership characteristics necessary to successfully navigate the fog of crisis and bounce back from adversity. The concepts were refined as the material was taught at the FBI National Academy and the Johns Hopkins Bloomberg School of Public Health. Over a decade later, with the passage of time and exposure to additional national and international adversity, including the COVID-19 pandemic, we felt it was time to look beyond merely bouncing back and to study the lessons learned about leadership aimed at "bouncing forward" to growth and transformation.

Our prescriptions are based on seven contributing elements: (a) a review of the oldest generally accepted classic treatises uniquely written during and about crisis leadership with an implied eye on transformation; (b) a review of selected works from the "golden age of leadership"; (c) our own research on presidential leadership in crisis from which tremendous transformations to American society ultimately arose; (d) the science of human resilience; (e) insights from recent discoveries in neuroscience; (f) exclusive interviews with some of the most noteworthy transformative leaders within their respective industries (and of whom you've probably never heard); and (g) the authors' direct observations of and research into the critical periods of uncertainty or adversity that have served as milestones for the last 50 years of Western history and that are greatly influencing our future, including the London Blitz, the domestic terrorism in Oklahoma City, the first Gulf War, the attack on the World Trade Center and the attacks of September 11, 2001, the SARS pandemic, the oil spill in the Gulf of Mexico, Hurricane Katrina, and the COVID-19 pandemic. From these experiences and more, the most salient lessons of transformative resilient leadership have been derived and distilled in this volume.

RESEARCH SUPPORTING OUR APPROACH: LESSONS FROM "THE HARDEST JOB IN THE WORLD"

John Steinbeck (1966) wrote, "We give the President more work to do than a man can do, more responsibility than a man should take, more pressure than a man can bear" (p. 46). Arguably, the study of American presidential leadership serves as a virtual proxy for all leadership roles but especially leadership under stress and adversity. The title of John Dickerson's (2020) *New York Times* best-selling book says it all: *The Hardest Job in the World: The American Presidency*. Dickerson made the case that the American president must be executive-, commander-, first responder-, and consoler-in-chief, in addition to being an "action hero." Dickerson concluded that the president must integrate and handle a wider variety of experiences than perhaps any other leader on the planet. Arguably, the study of American presidential leadership serves as a virtual proxy for all leadership roles but especially leadership under stress and adversity. The study of presidential leadership can teach powerful lessons about effectiveness and ineffectiveness in times of crisis.

So we decided to use presidential leadership as a proxy for leadership effectiveness overall, and especially as a proxy for resilience-focused crisis leadership. We found an exceptionally vast, robust survey of leadership experts that not only supports our model of the five pillars but also shows that resilience through adversity is viewed as the most critical determinant of overall leadership effectiveness.

Under the auspices of C-SPAN, a consensus panel of leadership experts was convened to identify core factors that predicted overall leadership effectiveness. The report was published over numerous years, most recently in 2021. The panel identified 10 core factors predictive of presidential leadership effectiveness (referred to as "the hardest job in the world"), but we believe they generalize to most leadership positions. The 10 core factors of leadership that C-SPAN identified were: communication and public persuasion, crisis leadership, economic/financial management, moral authority, international relations, administrative skills, relations with oversight or collaboration bodies, vision/agenda setting, pursuit of equal justice for all, and performance. We were curious as to the influence of these diverse variables. Understanding that these core elements were not equally predictive of overall leadership effectiveness, they were statistically analyzed and weighted as to their importance or overall predictive value. Of the 10 core elements of leadership, leadership in times of adversity and crisis was the most powerful predictor of overall leadership effectiveness when comparing the highest to the lowest performers (Hirdes et al., 2021). So we see that effectively leading through adversity not only resonates psychologically, it appears to be a critical empirical determinant of overall leadership effectiveness.

Everly et al. (2013) analyzed the C-SPAN presidential leadership surveys released in 2000 and 2009 (C-SPAN, 2000, 2009). We discovered that four factors, or what we refer to as "pillars," predicted overall leadership effectiveness. Our analyses yielded evidence that the most important and universally applicable leadership behaviors were (a) performance, what we refer to as decisiveness and action; (b) vision/agenda, what we refer to as an actively optimistic vision; (c) moral authority, what we refer to as a moral compass; and (d) public persuasion, what we refer to as effective communications.

C-SPAN replicated its survey in 2017, and we analyzed the combined results of this replicated survey and the two previous surveys (Everly et al., 2020). Using presidential leadership as a proxy for leadership in challenging situations, we contrasted the highest performing presidents against the lowest performing presidents, overall. We sought to identify the characteristics that best differentiated the two groups of presidents. We found the same four factors significant discriminators of high versus low presidential leadership effectiveness *overall* as assessed by C-SPAN's experts on leadership: (a) performance, (b) vision/agenda, (c) moral authority, and (d) public persuasion. A follow-up analysis of those data with the addition of C-SPAN's 2021 analysis caused us to add (e) fostering supportive relationships as a fifth pillar.

Can we now extend these findings of overall presidential leadership to crisis leadership? A final analysis of C-SPAN data (Everly & Athey, 2022; Everly et al., 2020) was conducted focusing just on crisis leadership based upon their report. We compared presidents who were highly effective leading during crises within their presidencies to presidents who largely failed to effectively lead during crises that existed during their terms in office. Let's look at the results:

Abraham Lincoln was rated by C-SPAN as the most effective crisis leader for his leadership during the American Civil War. He had a vision for a united country. He acted boldly and decisively. He was an expert communicator. He sought collaboration, even with his rivals, as documented by Doris Kearns Goodwin (2005) in her book *Team of Rivals: The Political Genius of Abraham Lincoln*. He was guided by a moral compass, even if his inclinations were unpopular.

George Washington was rated the second most effective crisis leader for his transformative crisis leadership during the American Revolution. Washington's vision for a new country was unparalleled, especially considering his refusal to be anointed "king" or accept a status of "president for life" when both were offered (a decision that prompted King George of England to call him the greatest man on Earth). His bold decision making was courageous. On December 25–26, 1776, Washington's army famously crossed the Delaware River and attacked roughly 1,400 Hessian troops camped around Trenton, New Jersey. His army was in desperate need of a significant victory over the British to bolster failing morale. The Delaware River was choked with ice, they were amid a winter storm, and the attack was delayed by 3 hours. Nevertheless, Washington persevered, and the attack was a success. Some argue this was a significant turning point in the war, as it showed the Americans to be capable of bold and unconventional action. As for moral authority, none of the "founding fathers" even approached his stature.

As for Franklin D. Roosevelt (FDR), his skills as a crisis communicator were without equal, except by Winston Churchill. But armed with more than words, he too acted boldly and courageously. He inherited a potentially catastrophic financial crisis from Herbert Hoover. Within the first days of his presidency, he risked impeachment by shutting down and "rebooting" the entire financial system of the United States. His famous radio "fireside chats" were initiated on a national level to inform and reassure his nation as they navigated through the Great Depression and World War II. As a direct result of the crises in his presidency, he established the foundations for a series of initiatives and programs that continue to improve life in the United States even today. Among those programs are the Farm Credit Administration, the Export–Import Bank, the Federal Deposit Insurance Corporation (FDIC), the Federal Housing Administration (FHA), the National Labor Relations Board, the Rural Utility Service (formerly the Rural Electrification Administration), the Securities and Exchange Commission (SEC), the Social Security Administration (SSA), and the Tennessee Valley Authority (TVA).

Finally, Theodore Roosevelt achieved that which had been deemed impossible. In 1902, he quelled the national mining strike that was paralyzing the entire country. In doing so, he engineered a resolution that satisfied mine owners, boosted the economy, returned a primary heat source to consumers, and gave new legitimacy to the nascent organized labor movement. In addition, understanding the ecological importance of his country's natural resources and a prescient eye to the future, Roosevelt initiated the national parks system. We can thank him for the preservation of beautiful natural resources we enjoy today.

As for the least effective crisis leaders, the C-SPAN studies identified three presidents as consistently the worst. James Buchanan was judged the most ineffective presidential crisis leader in American history for his failures to address the issues of slavery and secession. One month after he left office, the Civil War began. What were his failures? Buchanan failed to take the bold actions necessary to address the inhumanity of slavery and the potential dissolution of the Union threatened by Southern secession. Whether it was a lack of vision, indifference, or a lack of courage is unclear.

Andrew Johnson was rated the second least effective crisis leader. Johnson wanted a rapid restoration of the seceded Southern states to the Union but without protection for former slaves. This led to him becoming the first American president to be impeached. While he was acquitted by the Senate, it was by just a single vote. What were his failures? He acted without a forward-thinking vision informed by an understanding of history. He was willing to virtually ignore Lincoln's abhorrence of slavery and his subsequent legislative legacy in the form of the Emancipation Proclamation, as well as the fact that over 110,000 Union troops died in part to eradicate slavery. He acted without serious consideration for potential rapprochement through political coalitions.

Last, Franklin Pierce was rated the third least effective crisis leader by C-SPAN. Pierce, who preceded Buchanan, believed that the movement to abolish slavery was a threat to the unity and stability of the United States. In 1854, he signed the Kansas–Nebraska Act and was a supporter of the Fugitive Slave Act. Both actions further divided the nation and led to violent uprisings that foreshadowed the American Civil War. What were his failures? A remarkable lack of vision and a lack of courage to act boldly seemed to plague Pierce. According to the National Constitution Center (NCC Staff, 2021),

> The *New York Herald* marked his death with the following blunt statement: The 'deceased was a man of something more than average ability. He possessed, however, none of the attributes of greatness, and was more of a cautious, studious, and watchful politician than a comprehensive, far-seeing, or observant statesman.' (para. 2)

The actions of all three of these presidents selected by C-SPAN experts as the least effective crisis leaders are characteristic of shortsightedness, indecision, caution, and a general disregard for the consequences of their action or inaction.

The results of our analysis of the C-SPAN crisis leadership survey revealed five crisis leadership "pillars": (a) having a vision for success; (b) decisiveness in bringing that vision (mission) to life; (c) creating an environment of open, honest communications; (d) relationship formation; and (e) following a moral compass. These pillars clearly differentiated the most effective crisis leaders (Lincoln, Washington, Franklin D. Roosevelt, and Theodore Roosevelt) from the least effective crisis leaders (Buchanan, Johnson, and Pierce). While these findings are not definitive and are certainly subject to interpretation and debate, we find they add further support for our model and are consistent with both the "classical" lessons of history as well as the "modern classics" on effective leadership in crisis.

WHAT YOU WILL FIND IN THIS BOOK

In the corporate world, the "art of the turnaround," wherein a leader can snatch victory from the jaws of defeat, is one of the most valued of all leadership qualities. But perhaps there are universal lessons to be distilled from the sources enumerated above about bouncing back, bouncing forward, and even becoming a psychological promontory that resists the erosive forces of adversity. Whether it's a sports team, a business, a community, or even the way you live your life, there are recurring themes that predict success and serve as lessons for us all. This book describes those lessons and offers the stories of those leaders who have lived them.

Chapters 1 through 4 lay the foundation for our story by reviewing the most relevant classical and modern history, the science of human resilience, and principles of neuroscience as they apply to crisis leadership.

Chapters 5 through 9 describe the five pillars (characteristics) of transformative resilient leadership. Each chapter includes a simple self-assessment that allows you to assess and continually monitor your actions in each of these critical leadership domains. Throughout the book, we also highlight numerous profiles in transformative resilient leadership. Most of these are based upon exclusive interviews conducted with prime exemplars of transformative resilient leadership who have literally transformed their respective industries on national and international levels. In their own words, they give us concrete examples of how they shaped their organizations and industries fueled by adversity.

We would be remiss if we did not challenge and bring discussion to individual foundation elements of performance in the wake of stressful events: wellness. Chapter 10 briefly reviews the significance of self-care for the resilient crisis leader. Leaders are performers. And, at the end of the day, whether it is an acute response in crisis or sustaining high performance over time, leaders cannot perform if they are not well.

Finally, in Appendix A, there is a brief 10-item action agenda for the transformative resilient leader to use to help launch and subsequently guide the employment of core prescriptive principles: Action Agenda for Transformative Resilient Leadership.

We sincerely believe that when you reach the end of this book, not only will you understand transformative resilient leadership, but you will also be empowered to apply its principles. This book can empower CEOs, frontline managers, directors, teachers, coaches, parents, leaders of any kind, as well as those who study and aspire to any position of leadership, to create a *culture of resilience.*

I

FOUNDATIONS OF
TRANSFORMATIVE
RESILIENT LEADERSHIP

CHAPTER 1

STUDY THE PAST, PREPARE FOR THE FUTURE

Thou must be like a promontory of the sea, against which, though the waves beat continually, yet both itself stands, and about it are those swelling waves stilled and quieted.
—Marcus Aurelius, *Meditations*

The quest to find guidance, especially in uncertain or critical times, has been documented throughout recorded history, but what are the essential components of crisis leadership, especially crisis leadership with a transformative focus on growth-promoting resilience? To answer that question, we must embrace the Harvard philosopher George Santayana's (1905/2005) admonition "Those who cannot remember the past are condemned to repeat it" and begin our search almost 3,000 years ago.

LESSONS FROM THE CLASSICS

Our quest for the grail of transformative resilient leadership begins with what we refer to as the *classical treatises of leadership*. We have selected four that provide us with a historical foundation to understand not only leadership overall but especially crisis-oriented leadership—the best predictor of overall leadership and perhaps the most important predictor of the overall longevity of any group or organization. We specifically selected these four from myriad leadership guides because all four of these classical sources were specifically written during, or intended for, times of adversity and crisis with an eye to transformation and the future. They are, we believe, the earliest and most influential guides to transformative resilient leadership in Western literature.

Lessons From *The Iliad* and *The Odyssey*

The 8th-century B.C.E. Homeric poems *The Iliad* and *The Odyssey* (ca. 850–750 B.C.E./2011) tell the stories of the Trojan War and its aftermath. They relate the stories of heroes. The oral renditions of the poems likely predate the development of the written records by a century or two. Hellenic scholars generally agree that these stories may be the earliest recorded leadership lessons in literature, especially leadership lessons in times of crisis, although not specifically on transformative leadership. Nevertheless, we believe there are powerful lessons to be learned on transformation.

The Iliad details the Trojan War, which was fought between a coalition of Greek armies led by Agamemnon, king of Argos (Mycenae) and the army of the city-state of Troy. The war resulted from the abduction of Helen by Paris, prince of Troy. Helen was the wife of Menelaus and known in history as "the face that launched a thousand ships." Menelaus was king of Sparta and brother of Agamemnon. *The Iliad* tells the compelling story of the angst, conflicts, and tragedy that arise from the poor leadership of the self-absorbed Agamemnon. He is described as a great warrior and as such was considered worthy of leadership. Confusing technical skill with leadership ability is a mistake commonly made even now, 3,000 years later.

Homer portrays Agamemnon as an arrogant, self-absorbed leader lacking honor. His braggadocio was catastrophic, leading to the sacrificial death of his daughter, Iphigenia, enduring hatred from his wife, and his own murder. His narcissism led to a decline in morale among his soldiers and even a sense of betrayal that resulted in a near catastrophic rebellion within his ranks. History is replete with the stories of narcissistic leaders whose tenure in power ended catastrophically.

Homer teaches us early on that a truly great leader does not need to convince others of his greatness. The leader that does is often trying to conceal weaknesses in character. Homer warns us not only of narcissistic leaders but also to never underestimate the enduring anger and thirst for vengeance of those who feel betrayed. Machiavelli would echo this sentiment 2,200 years later, as would Abraham Lincoln, 300 years after Machiavelli.

Thus, Agamemnon's actions—based upon hubris, self-servitude, and a failed moral compass—serve as a virtual protype for poor crisis leadership, which has been replicated throughout history by leaders of governments, armies, and even modern corporations, as evidenced by the Gulf of Mexico's Deepwater Horizon oil spill in 2010, the 2008 financial collapse, and the political vitriol of the past decade.

Homeric stories are not without examples of effective crisis leadership, however. *The Odyssey* is the story of the Greek hero Odysseus and his journey to return to Greece to reclaim his throne as king of Ithaca after the Trojan War. It highlights the compassionate yet goal-directed leadership of Odysseus. He was committed not only to his own return but that of his followers in an arduous 10-year journey from Ilium. His journey was made perilous by crises brought about by adversaries who possessed far greater might or employed strategies of deception and even seduction. *The Odyssey* reveals the power of a constellation of leadership actions: (a) focused optimistic vision (keeping your eye on the prize); (b) decisive and tenacious guidance (making difficult decisions); and (c) thinking not only of oneself but embracing the obligation to actively protect, support, and lead those who follow, all while resisting the seductions and other temptations that power often brings. The leadership skills displayed by Odysseus and the foundational virtues upon which his leadership was built culminated in a successful return to a grateful wife and son and reascendence to his throne. *The Odyssey* serves as a virtual textbook of crisis leadership and human resilience. The serious student of crisis leadership is encouraged to read Hellenic scholar Gregory Nagy's (2013) masterful work *The Ancient Greek Hero in 24 Hours.*

Lessons from Sun Tzu's *The Art of War*

Written in the 6th century B.C.E., Sun Tzu's (ca. 500 B.C.E./1983) *The Art of War* is considered by many to be the most influential of the earliest texts on leadership in crisis. Most authorities believe Sun Tzu was a Chinese general, strategist, and philosopher. It is important to note that his strategic guidance was intended for a time of transformation. It was a time when the prevailing Zhou dynasty was weakened, and several feudal rulers were waging wars of annexation. The King of Wu hired Sun Tzu as an advisor on strategy. His influential text offers specific suggestions on how to prepare for and lead in times of crisis and war. Its lessons are deemed to have value in virtually all venues wherein leadership is exercised—its lessons are still taught from schools of business to the military academies and have relevance for the transformative resilient leader.

Sun Tzu extolled the virtues of (a) strategic thinking and preparation, (b) decisiveness, (c) following a moral compass, and (d) clear communications. He chastised the leader paralyzed by overanalysis or excessive caution and promoted the practice of decisive leadership amidst turmoil. He wrote: "Be decisive, vacillation saps the strength of any army. If action is necessary, make it swift, act boldly, no one benefits from protracted conflict or ambivalent leadership." He also extolled the virtue of morality, as it builds trust and a dedicated followership. He wrote: "When one treats people with benevolence, justice and righteousness, and reposes confidence in them, the army will be united in mind and all will be happy to serve their leaders." The Business Roundtable, a decade ago, noted the most resilient organizations advocate ethical conduct, especially in times of crisis when temptations to do otherwise are often very powerful.

Last, about the importance of open communications, he wrote, "If words of command are not clear and distinct, if orders are not thoroughly understood, the general is to blame." Over 2,000 years later, it was clear that lesson had yet to be learned. We recall the glory and the pathos of Lord Cardigan's disastrous charge of the Light Brigade on October 25, 1854, during the Crimean War, which still serves as one of the most egregious examples of failed communications in crisis. The British light cavalry was considered perhaps the best mounted military unit in the world, but a catastrophic communications failure led 600 troops into the wrong place, the "valley of death," and at the wrong time, from which only 125 returned ready to fight again.

The message for the crisis leader from Sun Tzu appears to be that in the fog of crisis (as in the fog of war), decisiveness, clear communications, and trustworthy actions are paramount.

Lessons from *The Prince*

Let us not forget the much-maligned Niccolò Machiavelli, whose treatise *The Prince* (Machiavelli, 1534/2006) is viewed by many as embracing treachery and deception as leadership tactics, although it may hold other more useful insights for even the most ethical of leaders. Written in the 16th century, *The Prince* is a transformative text. It was dedicated to Lorenzo di Piero de' Medici as a guide to princely leadership in a time of great opportunity. De' Medici ruled Florence in a time when Italy was divided into numerous city-states and fraught with uncertainty and regional conflicts. *The Prince*, some believe, was intended to be a guide for leadership in times of uncertainty and subsequent crises with the intention of assisting de' Medici in uniting Italy and creating the greatest Italy since the rule of the ancient Roman empire of Julius Caesar and Augustus (Octavius). Indeed, while *The Prince* does endorse behavior we deplore, he did advocate four principles we believe have relevance to crisis, human resilience, and growth beyond adversity:

1. Machiavelli advocated trusting observable behaviors, as people should trust actions more than words. This was perhaps derived from the words of Saint Anthony of Padua who said, "Actions speak louder than words" in a sermon he delivered in the early 1200s.

2. Machiavelli thought the study of history was important. He understood that abuse, marginalization, or neglect can lead to fomentation of hatred and revenge among those who have been defeated. The good will of the people, even the vanquished, is essential, as the conquering Roman legions understood. They worked to amicably integrate non-Romans into their empire. Machiavelli wrote, "For whoever believes that great advancement and new benefits make men forget old injuries is mistaken." Politicians, administrators, and leaders at all levels should heed this warning. This may be especially important for those leading in times of political polarization and vitriol.

3. He underscored the necessity to form collaborative alliances. Connection to others is a force multiplier. It divides sadness and multiplies happiness, as Cicero noted. Leaders should understand that coalition formation is based upon compromise.

4. Machiavelli advocated the value of acting in such a manner as to be "esteemed" and even beloved. "He who is highly esteemed is not easily conspired against. . . . Therefore, the best fortress is to be found in the love of the people, for although you

may have fortresses they will not save you if you are hated by the people." This was certainly exemplified by George Washington. Historians note that Washington's ethos and esteem were so great that he was considered above reproach during the tumultuous infancy of the United States. This was in stark contrast to the vitriol spewed between Thomas Jefferson and John Adams as they struggled for power.

Lessons from *Vom Kriege*

And last, we must mention Carl von Clausewitz's classic book *Vom Kriege* (*On War*; von Clausewitz, 1832/1984). Carl von Clausewitz was a Prussian general who fought against Napoleon and in other notable campaigns. *Vom Kriege* is considered essential reading for any student of leadership, as it is a key primer on strategic thinking. Strategy formation is the process of defining the vision by which one's expressed goals will be achieved. It is a high-level plan. Tactics, on the other hand, are the specific steps one must employ to bring a strategy to life. He recognized that communication is the essential process that converts strategy into action.

To von Clausewitz, the process of strategic thinking, especially in periods of uncertainty, is to pick the right engagements, be decisive at the right moment, be focused and tenacious, communicate the strategic vision, and foster a psychological advantage. The crisis of war is a trial of psychological and physical forces, he argued. From von Clausewitz's viewpoint, psychological factors are the ultimate determinants of effective leadership, especially in crisis and conflict. Borrowing from von Clausewitz's formulation, the crisis leader must understand that (a) effective crisis leadership is trinitarian: it consists of a conflict (crisis), people (followers, community members), and leadership, the latter two working together to overcome the first; and (b) resilience during and after crisis is an active process—equivocation, hesitation, and avoidance predict failure. In the final analysis, von Clausewitz believed that the combination of *integrity and strength* was the sine qua non of effective execution of strategy and effective leadership in turmoil. Hold that thought, for we explore it further in Chapter 2.

To repeat the aphorism of George Santayana, "Those who cannot remember the past are condemned to repeat it." So, what have we learned from the study of these four "classic" guides to transformative resilient leadership? History from the time of Homer through the Renaissance and the founding of the United States suggests the value of certain leadership attributes in times of uncertainty, crisis, and transformation. They are (a) a focused optimistic vision, (b) decisive and tenacious guidance, (c) supportive collaborative relationships, (d) effective communications, and (e) integrity. They typify the most effective leaders before, during, and after times of uncertainty, crisis, and even failure. Such leadership appears to (a) reduce uncertainty; (b) buffer the attacks of adversity; and (c) foster resilience, even growth. But it seems reasonable to assume that such attributes enhance leadership effectiveness in all circumstances, not just in crisis. Famed futurist Alvin Toffler once reflected upon George Santayana's admonition regarding history. In his 1972 book, *The Futurists,* he wrote, "If we do not learn from history, we shall be compelled to relive it. True. But if we do not change the future, we shall be compelled to endure it. And that could be worse." The best way to transform the future may be to embrace the lessons of the past.

THE BENEFITS OF ADVERSITY

Earlier, we indicated it is a rare leader who can not only lead to bounce back but to "bounce forward," achieving the transformative goal of growth-promoting resilience from the abyss of crisis. Is this an illusion, or can great growth follow great adversity?

The 5th-century Greek historian Herodotus (sometimes called the "father of history") famously told the story of the Egyptian phoenix, a bird that was reborn from its own ashes. The story has become an icon for the notion of rebirth. But it was the Roman Claudian several hundred years later who was the first say that the bird was reborn "more beauteous than before." So, we see perhaps the first mention in Western literature that growth can result from adversity.

In 1598, William Shakespeare penned the play *As You Like It.* One of the most famous lines from that play is spoken by the deposed Duke Senior, "Sweet are the uses of adversity which, like the toad, ugly and venomous, wears yet a precious jewel in his head" (II.1.12–1.17). Even 500 years ago, the potential value of adversity was recognized, not by a great healer, but by a great playwright. Can this really be the case?

Fast-forward to the great silent film era star Mary Pickford. She was called the most popular actor in the world in the 1910s and 1920s. Yet her acting career abruptly ended as a result of technology! Failing to successfully continue acting with the advent of the "talkies" (movies with recorded sound), she formed a powerful coalition with other talented stars and entrepreneurs of the era and cofounded the film company United Artists, which continues today. Shifting her talents to producing and directing, she became the most powerful woman in the entertainment industry. She created more enduring power than even at the height of her cinematic stardom. She also initiated a challenge to the monopolistic power held by large studios over performers. She once noted, "You may have a fresh start any moment you choose, for this thing that we call 'failure' is not the falling down, but the staying down."

Rather than fear the inevitability of adversity and crisis, a better tack would be to prepare for or even embrace it! As a muscle grows stronger with stress, so can teams, organizations, communities, and even individuals. Crisis reveals true strength. It also reveals true opportunities for those prepared to take advantage. With the dawning of the 20th century, the written form of the Chinese language largely changed to the logo syllabic Mandarin form. The English word "crisis" may be captured by the Chinese characters 危 机. Loosely translated, the first character may be considered the symbols for "danger." Numerous politicians, including President John F. Kennedy, Jr., and later Secretary of State Condoleezza Rice have suggested that the second symbol means "possibility" or opportunity. Yet, language scholars note that while the second symbol is a component of a word that means "opportunity," it is more likely that it means something closer to "change point." In any case, this rhetorical device highlights the power that can come when one considers the opportunities that crises may bring or the opportunity to shift and change to bounce forward, propelling not only individuals but communities forward.

Further, Dr. John Krumboltz's (2009) happenstance theory states that career and life development are best fostered by preparing for opportunities that you may not know even exist in the current moment. Many unpredictable factors are at work, potentially shaping the future. This includes crisis. One of President Obama's key advisors, Rahm Emanuel, once noted, "You never let a serious crisis go to waste. And what I mean by that it's an opportunity to do things you think you could not do before." Further, it may be said that a rising tide lifts all boats, but a storm can benefit the few that are prepared for adversity. Louis Pasteur observed, "Chance favors the prepared. . . ." In his last book, *Behold the Man*, the German philosopher Friedrich Nietzsche (1908) wrote that a person who has "turned out well" could be recognized by the ability to take advantage and prosper from adversity. Nietzsche wrote: "*Was ihn nicht umbringt, macht ihn starker*" ("What does not kill him makes him stronger"). Modern day sport psychologists

Fletcher and Sarkar (2012) have studied Olympic gold medal winners. They concluded:

> Exposure to stressors was an essential feature of the stress–resilience–performance relationship in Olympic champions. Indeed, most of the participants argued that if they had not experienced certain types of stressors at specific times, including highly demanding adversities . . . they would not have won their gold medals. (p. 672)

The Claudian description of the phoenix is the literary foundation for the psychological phenomenon known as posttraumatic growth. Richard Tedeschi and Lawrence Calhoun (1995, 2004) coined the term "posttraumatic growth." They noted:

> Posttraumatic growth is the experience of positive change that occurs as a result of the struggle with highly challenging life crises. It is manifested in a variety of ways, including an increased appreciation for life in general, more meaningful interpersonal relationships, an increased sense of personal strength, changed priorities, and a richer existential and spiritual life. Although the term is new, the idea that great good can come from great suffering is ancient. (p. 1)

Remarkable success stories after moments of great challenges and failures are countless.

Beyond the communities, we have numerous instances of the lives of legendary people being positively shaped by adversity. George Washington had a catastrophic leadership performance in the Franco–Indigenous War, but he later become Continental Army commander and president of the United States. Abraham Lincoln, who faced chronic depression, political failure, and the loss of a son, is consistently seen as the greatest American president. Harland Sanders developed the iconic brand Kentucky Fried Chicken (KFC) in his 60s while rebounding from a failed career as a lawyer. Al Neuharth experienced numerous unsuccessful attempts in publishing before founding *USA Today*. John Hershey created an entire town and an international empire around milk chocolate only after failing in his family's candy business. And Steve Jobs, who had his innovative technology company Apple taken from him by a hostile board of directors, regained control of the company, driving it to be the world's most recognized brand. There are thousands of other lesser-known people, whose lives were catapulted to greatness only having previously failed. General George Patton once noted, "I don't measure a man's success by how high he climbs, but by how high he bounces when he hits bottom."

Indeed, positive things can emerge from crisis. Transformative resilient leaders not only know this, but they also plan for it. In fact, we should be loath to find ourselves as overly protective leaders. According to two important books, *The Coddling of the American Mind* (2018) by Greg Lukianoff and Jonathan Haidt and *A Nation of Wimps* by Hara Estroff Marano (2008), overprotection is the greatest failure a society can commit toward its youth. It engenders a victim mentality and a false belief in fragility. And as Herbert Spencer wrote, the ultimate result of shielding men from their effects of folly is to fill the world with fools. Are we beginning to see those seeds bear fruit?

Courage is a necessary aspect of crisis leadership. One of the world's wealthiest men, Warren Buffett noted, "Be fearful when others are greedy and greedy when others are fearful." But as legendary investment strategist Sir John Templeton once said, "To buy when others are despondently selling and to sell when others are avidly buying requires the greatest fortitude."

Forged by the fires of adversity, crisis, and even disaster, for the keen observer there are powerful leadership lessons to be learned about how to avoid becoming a "victim" and certainly how to avoid leading others into the equivalent of Lord Cardigan's charge into the "valley of death." There are powerful lessons to be learned about how to be resilient and "snatch victory from the jaws of defeat," how to resist the pressures that bring others to their knees, and how to channel failures into opportunities for greater success than might otherwise exist. This is the essence of *transformative resilient leadership.*

KEY POINT SUMMARY

- Other than religion, leadership may be the most studied aspect of human behavior. Leadership is the ability to influence or guide others. It is the force that shapes social energy into a social force. It is the glue that keeps a team, an organization, or a society from dissolving into a chaotic crowd. Leadership can serve as a catalyst to help those who follow achieve things even they thought were beyond their reach.

- Four of the most esteemed and highly quoted guides to leadership were all written in times of crisis and turmoil. Each in its own way is not only a guide to crisis leadership but also a guide to transformative resilient leadership.

- The suggestions for leadership authored by Homer, Sun-Tzu, Machiavelli, and von Clausewitz when distilled appear to yield common denominators: (a) focused optimistic vision, (b) decisive and tenacious guidance, (c) supportive collaborative relationships, (d) effective crisis communications, and (e) integrity. These qualities appear to typify the most effective leaders before, during, and after times of uncertainty, crisis, and even failure. Such leadership reduces uncertainty, buffers the attacks of adversity, and fosters resilience with an eye of transformative growth.

- Resilient crisis leadership can be a competitive advantage that allows a leader to not only "snatch victory from the jaws of defeat" but also help those who follow grow stronger than they otherwise might.
- In sum, despite the angst of acute distress, adversity can not only be navigated, but it can also potentially lead to growth. Great good can come from great suffering. The goal of transformative resilient leadership is to not only "bounce back," it is to "spring forward!"

CHAPTER 2

MODERN CLASSICS

The "golden age" of modern leadership theory was roughly the period from 1960 to 1980. One of the most important of lessons to emerge from that era was an appreciation for "the human side of enterprise." Grounded in the writings of Abraham Maslow (1943), Douglas McGregor (1960), and David McClelland (1961), leadership theorists such as Fred Fiedler, Kurt Lewin, Robert Blake, and Jane Mouton asserted an immutable reality that leadership always consists of two essential roles: (a) to drive and support the mission (task function) and (b) to create an organizational environment that drives and supports the psychological well-being and investment of the workforce (psychological and relationship functions). The most effective leaders understand this duality of obligation and understand it is a dynamic process wherein some situations demand emphasis upon one role, while other situations demand emphasis on the other.

The duality of task and social leadership is often obscured in the fog of crisis and sometimes forgotten in military and other uniformed civilian services, including health care, because of rigid systems based upon rank. Dr. Hise Gibson reminds us of the importance of being mindful of the duality of leadership. Dr. Gibson is a colonel in the United States Army. He is a graduate of the United

States Military Academy West Point and holds a PhD from Harvard Business School. Despite stellar academic training, his current leadership on the faculties at West Point and at Harvard Business School, and numerous military deployments, he said it was a 15-month deployment to Iraq that underscored the importance of the duality of leadership:

> My time in Baghdad during Operation Iraqi Freedom shaped how I approach leading people. Just giving orders is not enough. As a leader, I had to focus on my soldiers. My unit had just left a year-long deployment in a combat zone, and I emailed my wife I would be home in 48 hours. In the midst of that email, I found out our deployment had been extended and I was returning to the combat zone. So, I had to tell her that I was returning to combat and did not know when I was coming home. Then I met with my unit. I had to be vulnerable. I shared what was going on, and after I shared why we were needed, why the nation required us and our expertise, and that our brothers and sisters had lost comrades over the past week, they understood why we had to return to Baghdad. We had to get back in the game. One misconception some leaders have is they just have to order people based on position (rank). It's a "do what I say and don't ask any questions" approach to leadership. There are huge problems with that. Especially since dealing with highly trained people, that would backfire. Although, sure, many would listen, they would all do exactly what I wanted, but we might have missed the opportunity to be innovative. If I just use positional authority, I know that would have really impeded our ability to be effective as a team. The key thing I've learned as a leader is the need for empathy and to take a moment to pause and be thoughtful before responding. It can really put a team at ease . . . ease anxiety and make a team more effective.[1]

---

[1]Interview with Dr. Hise Gibson, June 6, 2021.

THEORIES OF LEADERSHIP STYLES

This chapter reviews key leadership styles that emerged from the golden age of modern leadership theory. Core elements of these leadership styles are still viewed as critical for leadership today, as shown in a C-SPAN–supported study spanning several years. Table 2.1 summarizes these findings.

The Great Person Theory

Realization of the dual function of leadership has not always been the case. Leadership thought was once dominated by the *great person theory*. This approach to the study of leadership, which emerged in the 19th century, focused on the individual personality traits of leaders used to successfully engage, inspire, and empower their teams to be successful despite unbearable circumstances. Scottish philosopher Thomas Carlyle, writing in the 1840s, was an ardent supporter of this notion, which was later defended in 1880 by William James, one of the founders of American psychology. Key leadership traits were superior intellect, heroic courage, decisiveness, and perhaps even divine inspiration. A derivation of the great person approach to leadership is the charismatic leader. As the name denotes, such a leader attracts and guides followers on the strength of their charisma. They are often excellent orators. Given the well-being and success of the followership is dependent upon the charismatic leader, that well-being is jeopardized when the charismatic leader departs.

Theory X and Theory Y

In 1960, MIT professor Douglas McGregor published his classic, *The Human Side of Enterprise*. In that book, he described a bipolar conceptualization of leadership: *Theory X and Theory Y*. This

33

TABLE 2.1. Pillars of Transformative Resilient Leadership: Lessons From Modern Classics and C-SPAN Studies

Classics of leadership (emphasis on crisis, not resilience or transformation)	Servant/ transformational leadership (emphasis on transformation, not resilience or crisis)	Authentic and in extremis leadership (not a leadership style but leadership in a context)	Presidential crisis leadership (emphasis on crisis and transformation)
Optimistic vision	Vision for the future	Confidence, optimistic vision for future	Vision
Decisiveness	Decisiveness Risk taking	Decisive direction	Decisiveness/ performance
Integrity	Ethical action	High moral character	Morality
Communications	Communications		Effective communicators
Fosters cohesiveness/ supportive relationships	Supportive, collaborative relationships	Cohesiveness	Fosters relationships

Note. Data from a C-SPAN–supported study spanning several years (C-SPAN, 2000, 2009, 2017, 2021). Categories are provided by the authors and are not intended to match the C-SPAN categories.

conceptualization of leadership was framed within the context of motivational leadership. Theory X is authoritarian in nature. It relies upon a transactional system of objective-based punishments and rewards directed by the leader. For example, strategic planning and goal setting are the responsibilities of leadership. It is the responsibility of those who follow to achieve those goals. Psychological identification and investment reside in the *achievement* of the expressed goals as determined by leadership. Theory Y is more participative and democratic in nature. It asserts the best way to motivate others is by cultivating a psychological investment in workers through personal identification with the *product and the organization*. Psychological investment is fueled by autonomy, collaboration, and encouragement to innovate. Theory Y is to some degree predicated upon the implicit assumption that those closest to the work understand the work best. Different situations call for varying degrees of Theory X and Theory Y, some might argue, thus this formulation is dimensional.

Servant Leadership

In a seminal essay and subsequent elaborations, Robert Greenleaf (1970, 2002) described an extension of Theory Y that may be the first "modern" precursor to transformative resilient leadership. Greenleaf (2002) described a form of leadership wherein the leader's primary job is to serve:

> The servant–leader is servant first. . . . Becoming a servant-leader begins with the natural feeling that one wants to serve, to serve first. Then conscious choice brings one to aspire to lead. That person is sharply different from one who is leader first. . . . The difference manifests itself in the care taken by the servant first to make sure that other people's highest priority needs are being served. The best test, and the most difficult to

administer, is this: *Do those served grow as persons?* [italics added] Do they, while being served, become healthier, wiser, freer, more autonomous, more likely themselves to become servants? (p. 24)

Greenleaf's notion of the servant leader is a guide not only for operational leadership but also for ethical leadership. Servant leadership models as well as leading *in extremis* have gained considerable attention. In his book *The Servant Way: Leadership Principles from John A. Lejeune*, Maurice Buford outlined many of the servant leadership principles based on the life of the 13th Commandant of the United States Marine Corps (Buford, 2019). Overall, servant leaders are motivated to lead because of the desire to serve others and the organization. General Lejeune was identified as a man of great integrity and character. Lejeune amplified the value of moral character in life, and he emphasized this in his writings to the Officers of the Marine Corps (Lejeune, 1922) as he wrote, "Leadership is the sum of those qualities of intellect, human understanding, and *moral character* [emphasis added] that enables a person to inspire and control a group of people successfully."

The core characteristics of *servant leadership* are: (a) a commitment to the professional and personal growth of those who follow, (b) a commitment to build a sense of community, (c) a promise to take responsibility, (d) an optimistic vision, (e) the promise to listen empathically to those who follow, (f) the ability to promote the well-being of all, and (g) a commitment to one's own personal well-being. These core characteristics are strikingly like those uncovered from the "ancient" writers reviewed in Chapter 1.

Transformative Leadership

The concept of *transformative leadership* is generally credited to James MacGregor Burns (1978). He constructed the formulation after observing influential leaders within transformative political and social change movements. Such transformative leaders create a climate wherein leaders and followers prosper from reciprocal enhancement of motivation and growth.

In 1985, Warren Bennis and Burt Nanus penned the best-selling book *Leaders: The Strategies for Taking Charge*, in which they famously differentiated managers from leaders by noting managers do things right, while leaders do the "right thing." They argued that leaders express and foster a widely shared vision for the future. Leaders are decisive and take the risks that others wish they could but fail to take. Leaders show integrity and trustworthiness. Leaders assume the responsibility of communicating the organizational image and a coherent, compelling message. Last, leaders embrace transformative, collaborative, if not symbiotic relationships. Bennis and Nanus pointed to their work as likely serving as a platform for subsequent theory development of transformative leadership as it was subsequently applied to organizations.

Whether that speculation is correct or not, Bernard Bass's formulation *transformative leadership theory* shares similarities with the work of Burns and Bennis. Bass argued that transformative leaders provide an optimistic vision that rests upon credibility and trust granted by those they lead. Transformative leaders focus on their constituency, placing the collective above their own needs (Yukl, 2013). They achieve this end by exemplifying four characteristics:

- Individualized consideration: the degree to which the leader listens, encourages, and mentors others. The formation of supportive relationships between the leader and others is important.
- Intellectual stimulation: the degree to which the leader encourages and supports creativity.

- Inspirational motivation: the degree to which the leader inspires with optimistic communication and vision. "In order to foster supportive relationships, transformative leaders keep lines of communication open so that followers feel free to share ideas and so that leaders can offer direct recognition of each follower's unique contributions" (Bass & Riggio, 2005, p. 10).
- Idealized influence: the degree to which the leader provides a role model for pride of association and for ethical conduct.

Bass and Riggio (2005) noted that transformational leaders often respond more effectively in a crisis "because, unlike directive or transactional leaders who focus on short-term results and who may be prone to hasty, poorly thought-out decisions, transformative leaders are more likely to delay premature choices among options." (p. 63). Fiedler's cognitive resources theory (Fiedler & Garcia, 1987) shares that transformational leaders are often more effective under stress, as they are better prepared, organized, and rehearsed at their craft. This, in turn, relates further to their ability to respond with rapid, decisive leadership in times of crisis. Leadership that is relationship-focused has been shown to reduce feelings of burnout and symptoms of stress in professionals (Seltzer & Numerof, 1988). In sum, according to Bass (1998), "Transformational leaders . . . are those who stimulate and inspire followers to both achieve extraordinary outcomes and . . . develop their own leadership capacity." In that sense, transformational leaders function in the present with an eye to the future, but its expressed goal of classic transformative leadership is not that of leading through crisis to propel the organization and its people to a more prosperous future, per se.

Authentic and In Extremis Leadership

A leadership theory that includes elements of transformative resilience as we have previously identified them is *authentic leadership,* a form of transformational leadership. Authentic leaders model to followers authentic values, beliefs, and behaviors to transform the team dynamic or individual followers (Luthans & Avolio, 2003). Authentic leaders are deemed to be confident, optimistic, resilient, transparent, hopeful, future-oriented, moral/ethical, and center efforts to develop followers (Luthans & Avolio, 2003). Specific lessons for leaders to apply in developing their authentic leadership skill sets include defining purpose, values, focusing on relationships, and self-discipline (George, 2003). Authentic leadership, when practiced as being true to self and interpersonally authentic, can result in heightened trust in the leader, engagement, well-being, and sustained performance (Gardner et al., 2005). Last, extended authentic leadership models have built on processes such as trust and optimism. Research has supported key components, such as self-awareness, an internalized moral perspective, open communications, and relational transparency (Avolio et al., 2004).

A variation on the theme of authentic leadership is *in extremis leadership*. In extremis leadership is not a theory but a recognition of the unique context in which adversity, crisis, and life and death outcome may reside (Dixon et al., 2014; Dixon & Weeks, 2017). With in extremis leadership, leaders routinely place themselves in extreme danger and lead others in those circumstances (Kolditz, 2007). Kolditz (2007) noted that in extremis leadership is a leadership style that demonstrates (a) confidence, (b) optimism, (c) decisive direction, (d) high moral character, and (e) ethical reasoning. These leaders are most likely to create loyalty, obedience, admiration, and respect. Authentic leaders exert much of their effectiveness by making their followers feel safe. They ease fear and provide hope for those who follow; safety is based in trust, and trust in honor and integrity. In short in extremis leadership conveys the covenant of strength and honor in crisis.

Military leadership experts have highlighted the need for integration of authentic leadership, transformative leadership skills, and in extremis approaches in preparation for, during, and after dangerous action (Vogelaar et al., 2010).

In sum, varied aspects of modern leadership theories have indicated elements of leadership that can be used to promote transformative resilience in times of uncertainty and crisis. Ledesma (2014) conducted a review and noted that these elements include positive self-esteem, hardiness, strong coping skills, a sense of coherence, self-efficacy, optimism, strong social resources, adaptability, risk-taking, low fear of failure, determination, perseverance, and a high tolerance for uncertainty. While we may not all be working within a military in extremis condition, our working demands continue to evolve with fast-paced, uncertain, complex, and even volatile form. Adapting a working model for resilience-focused if not transformative crisis leadership may indeed save lives responding to non-combat demands. The crisis created by the COVID-19 pandemic of the 2020s exemplifies such a condition, wherein governmental and health care leadership were forced to make life-and-death decisions affecting both patients and health care staff.

Modern leadership thought owes much to authors such as Fred Fiedler, Robert Blake and Jane Mouton, Robert Greenleaf, Warren Bennis, and Burt Nanus, who pointed out the importance of the duality of leadership, pursuing the mission and fostering a supportive, collaborative, and resilient environment with a foundation of strength and honor. More specifically, they argued leaders should express and foster a widely shared vision for the future, demonstrate decisiveness, and take the risks that others wish they could (but fail to) take. They show integrity and trustworthiness, while assuming the responsibility of communicating the organizational image and a coherent, compelling message that serves both leaders and those who follow.

THE COVENANT OF LEADERSHIP

Leaders, in general and especially during crisis, make an implied if not expressed promise to not only lead but to lead with integrity. United States Army General George Patton is considered one of the greatest commanders of World War II. He once noted that the greatest failure in leadership is the failure to lead, especially in life-or-death crises. The words of Carl von Clausewitz (1832/1984) echoed and expanded this sentiment: "Leadership involves both performance and moral actions. In the final analysis, it is moral action that drives performance and as such it is the ultimate determinant of sustained effective leadership." Thus, von Clausewitz pointed to the notion that effective leadership, even crisis leadership in war, consists of attending to more than just the mission. Have you ever worked for a leader who could not make a decision, even in the best of times? Have you ever worked for a leader who became paralyzed in times of crisis? Have you ever worked for someone who said one thing then did another? Have you ever worked for a person who could not be honest, especially in stressful situations? A leader exhibiting any of these traits is usually ineffective at best, toxic at worst. Any of these traits will be viewed as a betrayal of a covenant (i.e., an implicit if not explicit agreement). As betrayal is one the greatest of human injuries, damage to the organization and to the overall morale of those who follow can be irreparable.

We assert that the covenant leaders make with those who follow is not only to lead but to lead with integrity guided by a sense of morality. We reframe this as the covenant of *strength and honor*. Strength most directly supports the mission. Honor largely supports the psychosocial aspects that undergird the pursuit of the mission (the "human" side of the enterprise). Strength and honor are two inextricably intertwined actions, neither of which can stand alone and yield the same impact. Strength and honor are not additive; we assert they are synergistic. In the spirit of full disclosure, this phrasing is borrowed from the Academy Award-winning movie *Gladiator* (Scott, 2000). Few would argue with the value of leading with strength and honor. To the seasoned leader such actions may emerge intuitively, but for the new leader, greater granularity is demanded.

As we recall from Chapter 1, five recurrent themes emerged as elements of transformative resilient leadership: (a) a focused optimistic vision, (b) decisive and tenacious guidance, (c) supportive collaborative relationships, (d) effective communications, and (e) integrity. The promise to lead with strength to support the mission and to further lead with integrity and honor to support the psychological needs of those who follow is merely a distillation of those five factors, or pillars. We believe the single most common mistake crisis leaders make is to focus solely on the mission while ignoring the psychological needs of their constituencies. This focus, while intuitively appealing in the short term, can be debilitating if the crisis becomes chronic and certainly in the quest for growth-promoting transformative growth in the wake of adversity.

Thus, we see an apparent convergence in the work of Homer, Sun-Tzu, Machiavelli, and von Clausewitz with Greenleaf, Bennis, Fiedler, and Bass around the covenant of strength and honor that leaders make to those who follow in crisis.

KEY POINT SUMMARY

- Effective leadership, especially transformative resilient leadership resides firmly in the balancing of mission-focused actions and actions focused on the well-being of those who follow.
- If we combine the lessons of leadership from history with the lessons of presidential leadership, we see the emergence of five "pillars" of effective crisis leadership: (a) having a vision for success; (b) decisiveness in bringing that vision (mission)

to life; (c) following a moral compass that presumably yields trust; (d) creating an environment of open, honest communications; and (e) forming networks for collaboration and mutual support.

- These five pillars are the core constituents of the covenant that each transformative resilient leader must make: *strength and honor*. These are the lessons we should ingrain in every potential crisis leader. This promise should serve not only as a virtual mantra but as the sine qua non of transformative resilient leadership.

CHAPTER 3

CRISIS LEADERSHIP THROUGH THE LENS OF RESILIENCE

Transformative resilient leadership is designed primarily to help *others* (those who follow) resist, adapt to, or rebound from crisis and adversity. It is a style of leadership that relentlessly searches for the opportunities for growth in adversity. It is a style of leadership that transcends leader-focused charismatic leadership to build a psychological culture that is not wholly dependent on the skill of the leader to be sustained. In many ways it may be considered a "legacy-focused leadership" style. Thus, an important foundation of transformative resilient leadership is psychological and neuroscience research on human resilience.

According to the National Academies' Institute of Medicine (IOM; 2013), "Resilient leadership practices serve as the catalyst that inspires others (the human resource) to exhibit resistance and resilience, and to exceed their own expectations" (p. 104). Further, "Resilient leaders can create the 'tipping point' that changes an entire culture" (p. 90). In this chapter, we examine what resilience is and why it matters.

THE NATURE OF HUMAN RESILIENCE

Have you ever known someone who had great aptitude but never lived up their potential? Have you ever known anyone who possessed profound knowledge or skill but, under pressure, failed to express it? Over the course of your life, your inability to be happy and achieve significant goals in your life is far more likely to result from a *lack of resilience* in the wake of adversity and failure rather than any other factor. One of the greatest life skills you can learn is resilience. And perhaps the greatest gift a leader can give to those who follow is the gift of resilience. Across disciplines you will find experts citing its importance. Coutu (2002) shared insights with business leaders on the critical role of resilience in individuals and organizations. One of her interviewees noted, "More than education, more than experience, more than training, a person's level of resilience will determine who succeeds and fails. That's true in the cancer ward, it's true in the Olympics, and it's true in the boardroom" (p. 47). Now, years later and with world crises piling up, we find many are quick to jump to noting the importance of resilience. Expert bloggers are capitalizing on the SEO strategies, and laypersons are commenting on how resilience can not only help us inoculate against mental illness but also boost performance. But, first, what is resilience?

According to Maria Konnikova (2016), writing in *The New Yorker*, the term "resilience" has been used in so many ways, it has lost its meaning. The generally accepted dictionary denotation is to bounce back, spring back, or recover after exposure to pressure or stress. That said, rather than a bouncing back from adversity, psychologist Dr. George Bonanno (2004) defined resilience as the ability of adults to maintain relatively stable and healthy levels of psychological and physical functioning after having been exposed to potentially disruptive or traumatic events. So, which is it? Is resilience the ability to be resistant to adversity (immunity), or is it the ability to bounce back from adversity? Efforts at reconciliation from the Johns Hopkins School of Medicine proposed that resilience is both and more.

Simply said, resilience consists of three factors, not one. Nucifora et al. (2007) argued that fostering the full range of resilience consisted of (a) building immunity (proactive psychological resistance) to stress; (b) fostering the ability to rebound (reactive resilience) from stress; and (c) using resilience in a transformative manner to not only bounce back but to bounce forward, higher than ever before. They went as far as to create *The Johns Hopkins Resistance Resilience Recovery (RRR) Continuum of Care* under the guidance of Dr. Michael Kaminsky, then vice chairman for clinical affairs. Building on our research, Kenneth Smith (K. J. Smith et al., 2018, 2020) sought to functionally clarify the definition using two advanced statistical techniques: structural equation modeling and confirmatory factor analysis. From his work, several findings relevant to our quest to use leadership to foster transformative resilience in states of crisis may be directly or indirectly derived: (a) poor leadership can contribute to stress and burnout; (b) leadership has the potential to mitigate stress and burnout; (c) resilience does indeed consist of at least two factors (resistance and reactive rebound), not one; and last, (d) resilience initiatives have the potential to reduce stress, burnout, and inclinations to quit one's job.

So, simply said, the answer to the question "What is resilience?" appears to be that resilience consists of the ability to withstand, bounce back, and even bounce forward, as growth can be spawned from crisis (Everly et al., 2015). Further, both leadership and resilience-focused initiatives have the potential to have a significant impact on an organization's climate and culture. This finding suggests that efforts to implement resilience-focused crisis leadership should therefore consider fostering those things that both build proactive resistance, enhance reactive resilience, and promote transformative growth.

THE CULTURE OF RESILIENCE

When a flower doesn't bloom, you fix the environment in which it grows, not the flower.

—Alexander den Heijer

Have you ever belonged to a team, a club, an organization, or some other group of people where not only were you proud to be a member but membership alone actually increased your self-confidence and motivated you to excel beyond your original expectations? It was an experience wherein membership and participation brought out the best in you, especially in the face of great challenges and even in the wake of adversity. As a member of the Rock & Roll Hall of Fame once said when questioned about his reluctance to retire due to ill health, "Have you ever been part of something greater than yourself?" There are indeed such entities that possess a legacy that empowers. We believe that such organizations of people, whether the organization is a place of employment (United States Supreme Court), a specialized form of training (U.S. Navy SEALs or U.S. Army Rangers), an athletic team (New York Yankees baseball, New England Patriots football, Alabama or Clemson college football), an educational institution such as a highly select school or university (Ivy League colleges, military academies), perhaps a family (de' Medici of Italy; Windsor of the United Kingdom; Grimaldi of Monaco; Rockefeller, Kennedy, and Mellon of the United States) or even a residential community (Palm Beach and Ocean Reef in Florida, Bel Air and Beverly Hills in California, "The Hamptons" in New York), could be environments or cultures with the potential to instill a powerful ethos and motivation to be more successful than you thought you could ever be, to seize crisis and turn it into opportunity, and if necessary, bounce back from failure to be stronger than ever before. This is what we refer to as a *culture of resilience*. Simply said, the culture of resilience may be defined as an environment wherein human resilience (the ability to withstand, or rebound, from challenges and adversity) is not only fostered but is embedded within the core fabric of the culture itself. The culture of resilience is characterized by cohesion, collaboration, pride in identification, and represents ideally a climate wherein growth is promoted, support is abundant, crisis is viewed as an opportunity, and the potential for innovation and growth is unlimited. Organizations most likely to survive and actually prosper in times of adversity possess a "resilient culture" and view crisis as opportunity, according to the IOM (2013) report on organizational resilience. Furthermore, former Assistant Surgeon General of the United States Dr. Brian Flynn once commented, "The only way to change an organization is to transform its culture" (personal communication, October 4, 2012).

CLIMATE AND LEADERSHIP

The question that must now be answered is, "How can the *culture of resilience* be created?" We envision this as a two-step process. The first step is to build an organizational climate of resilience. Dr. Joe Thomas (Ret. Lt. Col, USMC) is the director of the Stockdale Center for Ethical Leadership at the United States Naval Academy. Key to many of his teachings are issues of culture and climate. He noted, "Climate is the prevailing condition or set of attitudes that are established by leaders, and can be manifested in the behavior of people regardless of environment or occupation" (Thomas, 2016). Climate can be influenced by the mission or philosophy, the vision statement, and rules and regulations. Leaders integrating the key lessons of resilient crisis leadership into their own behaviors can start shaping the climate in their first interactions with others. Over time, the accumulation of these behaviors and resilient climate can have an impact on the culture.

This stepped process is significant as leaders can be empowered knowing that their behaviors can shape the direction of the organization's culture over time. Some refer to this process as "planting seeds and watering for growth." Unit-based leaders can also influence the resilient climate of their units regardless of the larger system's response. Disciplined resilience-focused crisis leadership behaviors will positively charge the climate, and over time the culture shift will lead to a resilient generational footprint.

Indeed, key here is the disciplined use of resilience-focused crisis leadership actions. As mentioned in Chapter 1, resilient leadership behaviors foster resistance to adversity, and when necessary, stimulate growth in the wake of crisis. Such growth can be at the personal, organizational, or community levels. IOM (2013) indicated that highly effective leaders can increase resilience to stressful conditions and may even lead to the creation of an entire culture of resilience that radiates to all aspects of the organization, and the community, as well. Resilient leaders can create the "tipping point" that changes an entire culture. That report goes on to note that training first-line managers to be resilient leaders may create that tipping point most efficiently.

THE NEED FOR RESILIENT LEADERSHIP IS INCREASING

According to United Nations, both natural and human-made disasters are increasing all over the globe. Economic instability has shown up in the most volatile financial markets in modern history. Trends in infectious disease reveal pandemics of greater or lesser severity emerging every decade. Certainly, not only did the COVID-19 pandemic send a devastating shock wave throughout the world, but it also changed the way people do business, where we reside, where we work, and generally how we live our lives, for at least this and the next generation. As the terrorist attacks of September 11, 2001, changed the world for the foreseeable future, so too will infectious disease. Resilience-focused crisis leadership should no longer be an interesting aspect of leadership training—it must be a mandated element in all leadership training, especially in government, public safety, health care, the military, and even education.

PERSONAL RESILIENCE

Before closing this chapter on resilience, we should mention personal resilience and growth in the wake of adversity. There appear to be three interacting forces that contribute to transformative personal resilience: sociological, psychological, and physiological.

From the sociological perspective, Dr. Emily Werner (2005) conducted a longitudinal study of at-risk youth on the island of Kauai. She discovered the most resilient of these young people had a supportive peer group and a mentoring nonparental adult in their lives. They actively sought trusted advisors or guides throughout their lives. The importance of this notion of interpersonal support and the transformative resilient leader is pursued in a subsequent chapter, but such support is imperative for personal resilience as well.

Psychologically, researchers from the University of Chicago examined the notion of personal "hardiness." Hardiness was a set of characteristics that helped one be "immune" to stressful conditions. Lead researcher Suzanne C. Kobasa (1979) operationally defined hardiness as the combination of three factors: (a) *commitment*, that is, personal involvement not merely participation in one's experiences; (b) *control*, that is, the belief in one's ability to effect some control in one's life; and (c) *challenge*, that is, the belief that change can be positive. People who were characterized with high hardiness experienced fewer stress-related diseases/illnesses, even though they may find themselves in environments laden with adversity and crisis. In their book *Stronger: Develop the Resilience You Need to Succeed*, Everly et al. (2015) reported similar findings based on interviews conducted with highly resilient U.S. Navy SEALs, medical patients, and professional athletes. They found that optimism, decisiveness and control, tenacity, a moral compass, and interpersonal support were characteristics predictive of personal resilience and even growth in the face and wake of adversity.

Last, physiologically, as a musical instrument can be tuned sharp and overresponsive, it can also be tuned down to be less reactive. So, too, can your nervous systems be "tuned." Based on elegant research investigations, physiologist Ernst Gellhorn (1968) concluded that human nervous systems are capable of being "tuned" so as to be irritable, hypersensitive, and overresponsive as well as "tuned" to be calm and almost imperturbable. This notion was proven in the early 1980s by J. W. Hoffman and others at a research laboratory at Harvard Medical School. The results, published in the prestigious journal *Science* (Hoffman et al., 1982), demonstrated that consistent practice of the "relaxation response" could actually create reduced physiological responsivity to stressful events. After being trained in the relaxation response (mantra meditation), subjects showed evidence of lower reactivity of the nervous system to stressful challenges. This effect is like the effect of antiarousal beta-blocker medications. Practicing mindfulness (i.e., focusing on being in the present) and relaxation response training appears to help create resilience at the physiological level.

KEY POINT SUMMARY

- Over the course of your life, your inability to be happy and achieve significant goals in your life is far more likely to result from a *lack of resilience* in the wake of adversity and failure than from any other factor.
- Resilience consists of the ability to withstand adversity, bounce back from crisis, and even use adversity and crisis transformationally.

- The term *transformative resilient leadership* is a legacy-focused leadership style consisting of those leadership behaviors that are designed to primarily help *others* (those who follow) resist, adapt to, or rebound from crisis and adversity by building an organizational culture of resilience.
- The only way to affect lasting changes in an organization is to change its culture.
- An organizational culture of resilience represents an environment or culture that has the potential to instill a powerful motivation to be more successful than you thought you could ever be, to seize crisis and turn it into opportunity, and if necessary, bounce back from failure to be stronger than ever before.
- Building an organizational climate of resilience may be a necessary first step for the resilience-focused leader. Climate is the prevailing condition or set of attitudes that are established by leaders and can be manifested in the behavior of people regardless of environment or occupation. It approximates the culture.
- Training resilient leaders, especially frontline leaders, is the best way to create an organizational culture of resilience.
- Personal resilience can be created through sociological, psychological, and physiological interventions. Developing supportive interpersonal networks, hardiness, and practicing mindfulness and relaxation techniques have all been shown to foster personal resilience.

CHAPTER 4

ESSENTIAL NEUROSCIENCE FOR LEADERS

You have only 7 seconds to solve the following problem. Ready, go! If it takes 10 workers 10 minutes to solder a total of 10 electrical connections, how long would it take 100 workers to solder a total of 100 electrical connections? Quick, what's your answer? Hold that thought.

—This challenge is based on the work of
Shane Frederick (2005).

Have you ever asked an otherwise capable person to do something simple during a high-pressure situation, yet found they were unable to comply, even after they said they understood? Have you ever seen an otherwise competent leader who was simply unable to make good decisions under pressure? Perhaps they were simply unable to make *any* decision at all—seemingly paralyzed in the midst of a crisis. The failure to lead effectively in a crisis can sometimes be traced back to a failure of the leader to understand how stress affects the brains of those who follow and thus their capacity to understand and follow direction. Failure can also result from the inability of the leader to understand that their *own* capacity to process information, innovate, and make effective decisions in the midst of adversity may become reduced.

This chapter reviews what leaders should know from the study of neuroscience. Leaders must know what a person can and cannot do in a crisis state. Leaders must know what constitutes realistic expectations versus unrealistic expectations concerning performance, information processing, and the ability to carry out leadership directives under stress.

Many people have understood the revolutionary impact that technology has had on the world over the last 30 years. However, there is another revolution that is going on quietly at the same time—one that is reshaping our understanding and practice of crisis leadership. That revolution resides in neuroscience. In this chapter, we describe the latest credible revelations from neuroscience that affect transformative resilient leadership. But first, let's review the basics.

BASIC NEUROBIOLOGY

The human brain has about 100 billion nerve cells, each with 3,000 to 7,000 synapses—around 700 trillion total connections. These connections form a neurological fabric that is the biological foundation for all thought and emotion. Like any fabric, this neurological fabric has basic "woven" patterns that dictate its functional strengths and its weaknesses.

With every thought, felt emotion, and active behavior, you temporarily modify the physiology of your brain. However, with the repetition of those thoughts, emotions, or actions, you not only modify your brain's physiology, but you also begin to modify your brain's functional structure. This amazing ability of the brain to reorganize itself is called *neuroplasticity*. The greater the number of repetitions, the greater the tendency to rewire your brain. Physiologist Donald Hebb (1949) once noted that brain cells that fire together, wire together. Neuroplasticity is the basis for learning any motor action, such as riding a bike or swinging a baseball bat. It is also the process underlying the acquisition of new knowledge. The more you study something, the greater the likelihood you will retain it. One of the most famous examples of this reorganizing ability is the finding that the hippocampi (the part of the brain that is involved in short-term memory, directional awareness, and problem solving) in London cab drivers were much larger than those of London bus drivers who simply followed the same route every day (Maguire et al., 1997). Neuroplasticity can also underlie repetitive thought patterns and emotional reactions, both positive and negative. The brain is extremely malleable, capable of changing its shape and function. It can also change its inclination to activate certain pathways. Think of that as *excitability*. The process of changing the excitability of functional patterns of nerve cells is known as *tuning*. As a musical instrument can be tuned to be sharp and highly responsive, or dull and underresponsive, so too can the brain be tuned to be overresponsive or underresponsive. Irritability and an exaggerated startle response can be early warning signs of an overly responsive excitatory tuning process being initiated. The agent process of change is repetitive neurological stimulation. Neurological repetition is not only facilitated by (a) conscious effort, but it can also be a result of (b) the environment (the physical environment as well as psychological climate and culture) wherein one lives and/or works, and even (c) natural intrinsic inclinations the brain possesses.

STRESS AND THE BRAIN

Stress is the brain's natural defense system. It is often referred to as the "fight or flight" response, now updated to the "fight–flight–freeze" response. This term was coined by Nobel Laureate Dr. Walter Cannon. He described this survival mechanism in his book, *The Wisdom of the Body* (1932). Cannon detailed an elaborate self-defense mechanism involving the amygdala (an almond-shaped pair of structures residing near the middle of the brain's inner core) and its effector response system is the sympathetic nervous system resulting in the release of the hormones (activator) adrenalin and cortisol, among others. Dr. Hans Selye called this response the "stress response" and wrote about it in his book *The Stress of Life*, published in 1956. The hormones better prepare you to survive threats to your survival. The advent of the Industrial Revolution saw the triggering mechanisms for the stress response dramatically shift from physical life-or-death threats to psychological threats. Perceived threats to one's status, competence/self-control, sense of fairness, meaningful relationships, and even threats to predictability/certainty are all capable of triggering a stress response that can rival the intensity of a threat to one's life. The stress response, when experienced chronically or at highly acute levels, can lead to physical illness. It is important for the leader to understand that in periods of high stress, the priorities of the human brain and body shift to physical survival. It will even do things to survive in the moment that are self-destructive in the long run.

SIX INTRINSIC INCLINATIONS OF YOUR BRAIN

In this section, we review six intrinsic inclinations the brain possesses that can affect both leaders and followers in crisis. See if you can think of an example of each of these you have seen in your personal or professional life.

1. THE BRAIN IS NATURALLY NEGATIVE, AND STRESS ACCENTUATES THIS INCLINATION

The brain is endowed with greater sensitivity to unpleasant news than to positive news. Neuropsychologist Dr. Rick Hanson said, "Our brains have become like Velcro for negative experiences and Teflon for positive ones." The predisposition is called the "negativity bias" (Ito et al., 1998) and is so automatic that it can be detected in the earliest stages of brain information processing (as early as the first year of life). The brain encodes negative experiences in long-lasting memories in less than a second. The encoding of positive experiences takes 10 to 12 seconds. The 5:1 Rule posits it takes five to 10 positive results to balance a negative. According to seminal research on human relationships, to maintain a happy marriage, each negative interaction must correspond to five positive ones (Gottman & Levenson, 2002). It has been suggested that in leadership, it takes five positive comments to balance one negative comment.

2. The Brain Relentlessly Searches for Threats

To maximize chances of survival, the brain constantly scans the environment for threats. It is prone to anticipate the emergence of threats not yet in evidence and to see threats not actually there. These inclinations can be seen as extensions of the negativity bias described previously and become more pronounced in a crisis. The lack of effective leadership-initiated crisis communications creates an information void that sets the stage for enhanced scanning. The more one identifies threats, real or imagined, the greater the inclination to continue to scan the environment and to identify even more threats, real or imagined, based on the neuroplasticity just described. The absence of timely, transparent, and truthful communications serves to fuel this inclination. The net result is often that the leader loses control of the actions of the followers. A group can become an unruly mob. The lesson for the resilient crisis leader is that timely and truthful communication is essential in a crisis. This takes us to the next inclination.

3. The Brain Is Programmed to Worry

Given the slightest provocation (or even just left to its own devices), the brain initiates a reiterative process of concern commonly referred to as *worry*. Using a statistical technique known as structural equation modeling designed to create causal models of human behavior, our own research conducted over 30 years has confirmed worry to be potentially toxic to human health, to feelings of satisfaction, and to professional stability (K. J. Smith et al., 2012). More specifically, burnout (mental and physical exhaustion) fueled by worry was seen to predict low job satisfaction, low job performance, inclinations to change jobs, and even inclinations to use unacceptable accounting practices by financial auditors. The brain possesses two mechanisms by which it is inclined to worry. First, psychologist Dr. Mihaly Csikszentmihalyi (1997) contended that unless we are occupied with activities or focused on other thoughts, worrying is the brain's default position. Worry, the repetitive preoccupation with negative thoughts, has been shown to increase the release of stress hormones, which can accelerate the aging process and otherwise predict stress-related physical illnesses (Everly & Lating, 2019).

The second mechanism by which worry emerges is in response to real or threatened adversity. Even Freud recognized a repetitive propensity of the human brain when confronted with and awakened by extreme adversity and trauma. The brain can become tirelessly obsessed with problems. The brain will play the problem repeatedly until it solves the problem or releases the problem as no longer important. Sadly, with some serious problems, this release can take days, months, years, or may never occur. The overly intense or chronic release of the stress response hormones that often accompanies traumatic life experiences is associated with anxiety, depression, and stress-related physical illnesses (Brosschot et al., 2006; for a review, see Everly & Lating, 2019). It also fuels future inclination to worry via neuroplasticity.

For the crisis leader, this underscores the importance of timely and truthful communication, ideally containing an optimistic future-oriented vision, as these will likely mitigate inclinations for worry. Data from structural equation modeling research (K. J. Smith et al., 2020) suggest that leadership practices and efforts to foster resilience within organizations may reduce stress, burnout, and inclinations to quit one's job, while improving job satisfaction. Similarly, resilience could reduce stress and burnout (K. J. Smith et al., 2015).

4. Stress Associated With Urgency and Crisis Can Reduce Your Ability to Solve Problems and Can Lead to Catastrophic Mistakes

The forward-most part of your brain is called the prefrontal cortex. This is where cognition (thinking) and related executive functions such as problem-solving reside. Psychologist Dr. Daniel Kahneman, winner of the Nobel Prize in Economics, has researched cognitive states for more than 4 decades. Based on the work of Seymour Epstein, Kahneman identified two systems for cognition: the dual model he referred to as System 1 (fast) thinking and System 2 (slow) thinking (Kahneman, 2011).

System 1 thinking is intuitive. It is fast, automatic, frequent, emotional, and impulsive. It is binary in nature. It uses energy-conserving cognitive shortcuts such as assumptions and biases to fill in informational gaps based on one's prior experiences. It does not employ working memory, which is necessary for solving novel problems. Although this intuitive cognition is the brain's preferential mode of thinking due to its speed and low glucose utilization, it is very often wrong. The error rate for decisions made under stress are estimated to range from 30% to 75% (Devilbiss et al., 2012; Grantcharov, 2019; Tay et al., 2016).

System 2 thinking, on the other hand, is deliberate and rational. It is slow, effortful, logical, calculating, and dimensional (as opposed to binary), so it sees the world in shades of gray. It employs working memory as a means of innovating and solving problems. System 2 thinking requires high levels of glucose. Stress interferes with System 2 rationale thinking. Distractions, physical exhaustion, hunger, time urgency, and emotions such as depression and anger also interfere with System 2.

Reliance upon intuitive System 1 thinking is exaggerated under stress. In fact, it can be said that System 1 hijacks System 2 in periods of crisis, stress, and adversity. This has been referred to as the "dumbing down phenomenon" and explains "why smart people do dumb things." System 1 can lead to sometimes catastrophic impulsive actions such as panic retreat, road rage, airline rage, and the like. The stress hormones adrenalin and cortisol are partially responsible for the System 2 to System 1 shift and can even result in damage to brain cells if activated for extended periods of time or at very high intensity levels, a process known as *neurotoxicity* (Everly & Lating, 2019).

Leaders should be aware that System 1 thinking may impede the ability of subordinates to solve problems and follow directives. Crisis as a psychological context or environment characterized by urgency, ambiguity, fear, and turmoil is a critical factor hindering effective communications, as we shall see in Chapter 7. It affects the leader's ability to make decisions and the followers' ability to respond effectively to those decisions.

Last, discovered as a result of combining numerous brain mapping studies (Shulman et al., 1997), the *default system* is activated during moral reasoning and understanding the perspectives of others (perspective taking). It is believed that the default system is generally active in fantasy, imagination, daydreaming, and aspects of creative thought, as well (Buckner et al., 2008). It is believed that stress and worry associated with crisis act to interfere with one's ability to empathize, understand the actions of others, and follow a moral compass. This inclination may not only interfere with a leader's ability to empathize with others and make decisions but also the ability of leaders and followers to act with honesty and integrity.

So, at the beginning of this chapter, we asked a question: If it takes 10 workers 10 minutes to solder 10 electrical connections, how long would it take 100 workers to solder 100 electrical connections? System 2 thinking would reveal the answer to be 10 minutes. But under the stress of urgency, System 1 thinking would lead you to believe the answer is 100.

5. THE BRAIN MAKES ASSUMPTIONS

There is no such thing as an information vacuum. If the brain does not receive essential information, it creates it. In situations of uncertainty and ambiguity, the brain fills in the blanks so that the situation makes sense. The gaps are filled with information based on (a) past experiences, (b) your greatest hopes, or (c) your greatest fears. Crisis leaders must remember resilience is based on a sense of empowerment, whether direct or vicarious (Bandura, 1997). Francis Bacon once reportedly said, "Information itself is power." The leader who fails to communicate in a crisis risks losing the ability to lead.

6. THE BRAIN HATES SURPRISES; IT NEEDS PREDICTABILITY

The stock market likes predictable situations; the brain does too. One of the most toxic cognitive conditions occurs when the reality experienced is incompatible with the reality expected. The septo-hippocampal system within the brain's limbic system (the same system wherein the amygdala resides) has been called the *great comparator*. It compares experience with expectation. When they match, stress levels remain low. When there is discordance or incompatibility, anxiety, frustration, and anger result (Gray, 1982). This compromises the leader's ability to make decisions and the ability of others to follow. This fact underscores the importance of planning, preparation, and practice (rehearsal). Crisis leaders must anticipate adversity while preparing accordingly. Marco Sala, CEO of International Game Technology (IGT; see Chapter 6), the largest gaming company in the world, provided us with two critical insights: (a) leaders must go so far as to try to anticipate even the things that are the hardest to imagine, and (b) sometimes a leader simply has to act, you cannot wait for the moment of absolute certainty. Forewarned is forearmed.

The wise crisis leader necessarily focuses on resilience. Resilience is fueled by being forewarned about inclinations and intrinsic limitations as they pertain to oneself and those who follow. Knowledge of these factors allows the leader to set appropriate expectations and best plan for overcoming such factors as may hinder effective performance.

REWIRING YOUR BRAIN: NEUROLOGICAL OVERWRITING IS THE KEY

Researchers from diverse fields ranging from the building of self-efficacy (Bandura, 1997) to the treatment of trauma (Everly & Lating, 2019) have argued that planning, preparation, and the consistent practice of empowering responses can be effective in not only reducing disabling stress but also rewiring the brain to respond extremely effectively in crisis. If crisis leaders understand these natural inclinations, they can better prepare not only to lead in crisis but also to foster resiliency.

The good news is that the same neuroplastic and tuning mechanisms that bias us to make poor decisions can be harnessed to reverse those self-defeating patterns (for a review, see Everly & Lating, 2019). Neuroplasticity can be harnessed to make our decision making less vulnerable to crisis-induced errors. A process we shall refer to as *overwriting* appears to be the key. From the perspective of information processing, overwriting refers to the process of creating new information and functionally superimposing it on preexisting information. Overwriting may consist of two processes: (a) the creation of competing information pathways that with time and use subordinate the preexisting pathways or (b) utilization of the same characters or infrastructure to erase any trace of the preexisting pathways. So powerful are these mechanisms, we believe they may even be capable of overriding some genetic programming.

Focused thought and repetition are the keys to effective crisis decision making. Focused thought and repetition over time are the keys to rewiring your brain, as well. Clearly, repetition appears to be the most powerful way of overwriting to reduce vulnerability to the threats enumerated above. There is a popular belief that it requires 10,000 hours to achieve this level of rewiring. This assertion has been challenged, however. Certainly, the level of effort associated with overwriting will vary across tasks. Biologically, we believe we understand the chemistry of creating enduring neural patterns. Thoughts and behaviors are seared into the structure of your brain by either highly intense stimulation resulting in high quantities of norepinephrine and/or glutamate being released, or sufficient repetition to cause the rewiring and "sealing" of neural pathways through the release of gamma-aminobutyric acid (GABA). These notions are still speculative but intriguing nonetheless.

Last, one of the most exciting revelations concerns the potential acceleration of learning using supplements. In the science fiction movie *Limitless* (Burger, 2011), a man dramatically increased his intelligence by taking a pill. Though no "limitless pill" exists, researchers have begun to find ways to chemically enhance learning. Jennifer Forsyth et al. (2015) presented evidence that increasing excitability at the glutamate N-methyl-D-aspartate receptor (NMDAR) on postsynaptic neurons can accelerate learning. They stated, "This suggests exciting possibilities for manipulating plasticity in adults using glutamatergic NMDA receptor stimulant D-cycloserine (DCS)" (p. 15331).

THE IMPORTANCE OF PERSISTENCE

Persistence serves two essential functions: (a) it fuels neurological overwriting and (b) it increases the likelihood of successful outcome once a decision has been made. Persistence can be the difference between success and failure. The visionary hotelier Conrad Hilton once noted, "Success seems to be connected with action. Successful people keep moving. They make mistakes, but they don't quit."

Calvin Coolidge was the 30th president of the United States, most remembered for bringing integrity back into government after the scandals of the Warren Harding administration, including the infamous Teapot Dome and Veterans' Bureau scandals. Perhaps his three most famous quotes are: "The chief business of the American people is business," "Leaders should not expect to build up the weak by bringing down the strong," and the following quote on persistence:

> Nothing in the world can take the place of Persistence. Talent will not; nothing is more common than unsuccessful men with talent. Genius will not; unrewarded genius is almost a proverb. Education will not; the world is full of educated derelicts. Persistence and determination alone are omnipotent. The slogan "Press On" has solved and always will solve the problems of the human race. (Shapiro, 2006, p. 173)

Regarding persistence, one simple fact seems immutable. The leader who quits will never know how close they came to success. That said, the admonition to never give up is not as simply employed as it may seem. We are not saying that leaders should be blindly persistent at all costs. We are reminded of the notion that irrationality is often defined as repeating the same actions expecting a different outcome. Leaders should always engage in an evidence-based cost–benefit analysis. That is, the effective leader, especially one who is focusing on resilience in the midst of crisis, when time and resources may be limited, must always assess the cost of continuation versus the anticipated outcome of continuation, while constantly monitoring any evidence of incremental improvement or regression.

Remember in Lewis Carroll's *Through the Looking Glass* (1871) when Humpty Dumpty scornfully tells Alice that words mean whatever he wants them to mean? When Alice questions him on whether or not he can do such a thing, he simply replies, "The question is, which is to be master—that's all." The biology of our brains, with their engrained energy saving defense mechanisms, are not the master. Instead, the brain is a tool waiting to be harnessed. The question is which is to be the master: the brain or its user? Through resilience-focused crisis decision making, we can better realize the power of this tool.

KEY POINT SUMMARY

- The failure to lead effectively in a crisis can sometimes be traced back to a failure of the leader to understand how stress affects the brains of those who follow (and thus their capabilities) as well as those who are led (and thus their capacity to make effective decisions).

- With every thought, felt emotion, and active behavior, you temporarily modify the physiology of your brain. However, with the repetition of those thoughts, emotions, or actions, you not only modify your brain's physiology, but you also begin to program your brain's functional structure. This process is called *neuroplasticity*. Inconsistent leadership, a lack of leadership, and anxiety- or fear-provoking environments may have the effect of programming a diminished capacity to function effectively in crisis for both leaders and those who follow.

- The stress associated with crisis interferes with rational thought, problem solving, empathy, and moral reasoning. It can result in a paralysis in decision making, System 1 intuitive thought hijacks System 2 rational thought. The result can be lapses in rational judgement leading to catastrophic decisions or paralyzing indecisiveness.
- System 1 cognition can lead to poor decisions approximately 30% to 75% of the time. It can also lead to highly risky impulsive actions.
- Resilience-focused leadership must acknowledge the neurologically based risks inherent in highly stressful circumstances and respond by
  a. practicing the 5:1 principle (it takes five positive comments to equal one negative);
  b. communicating in a timely and truthful manner;
  c. planning, preparing, and practicing responding to crisis and adversity to override tendencies to overreact, under-react, or act impulsively in such times;
  d. recalling Marco Sala's advice to avoid paralyzing anxiety and confusion triggered by the unanticipated: (a) leaders must go so far as to try to anticipate even the things that are the hardest to imagine, and (b) sometimes simply act based on one's best judgement—you cannot wait for the moment of absolute certainty; and
  e. remembering the only failure in crisis is the failure to lead. In crisis, the minds of those who follow usually search for guidance. If it does not come in a timely manner, the leaders have abdicated their leadership and a group becomes a disjointed crowd, or worse yet an angry mob.
- Neuroplasticity can be harnessed to make our decision making less vulnerable to crisis-induced errors. A process we refer to as "overwriting" is the key. Overwriting refers to the process

of creating new information and functionally superimposing it on preexisting information. Overwriting may consist of two processes: (a) creation of competing neuronal information pathways that with time and use subordinate the preexisting pathways, or (b) utilization of the same neuronal infrastructure that serves to erase any trace of the preexisting pathways. Focused thoughtfulness and repetition are the keys to overwriting self-defeating inclinations in crisis and instilling more effective crisis decision making.

- Persistence is a key resilience-focused attribute. It fuels neurological overwriting and increases the likelihood of successful outcome once a decision has been made.

II

THE FIVE PILLARS
OF TRANSFORMATIVE
RESILIENT LEADERSHIP

CHAPTER 5

OPTIMISTIC VISION

Perpetual optimism is a force multiplier.

—General Colin Powell

In 2020, we witnessed leaders step up to challenges with an optimistic vision while others struggled or even panicked in trying to formulate an organizational response to the COVID-19 pandemic. Higher education, like many industries, faced unprecedented challenge in keeping their communities healthy and safe to maintain operations. Dr. Jane Hunter, vice president for strategic initiatives at the University of Arizona, and her team rose to the challenge to develop sophisticated, state-of-the-art solutions in response to the COVID-19 crisis.

Dr. Hunter was not new to developing innovative solutions to a dynamic, complex problem set. In addition to leading projects designed to improve the quality of education at the University of Arizona, she serves as chief of learning solutions for Skeens McDonell Consulting Group, where she develops and conducts project management and leadership training programs and provides professional services to organizations striving to maximize the performance of their project teams. She holds degrees in mechanical engineering, engineering management, and higher education.

As the nation developed a better understanding of the disease, the senior leadership of the university realized that it would not be feasible to prepare for a campus reentry for fall 2020 unless all of the proper public health measures were put into place. Large working groups and smaller subgroups were formed, including the Test Trace Treat (T3) Teams and the Reentry Implementation Planning Teams. The provost asked Hunter to lead this diverse group of leaders from units across the university to develop strategic and operational plans to prepare for reentry. Although Hunter and her team had limited experience in the medical and public health fields, outstanding project management and leadership skills enabled them to guide quickly and effectively the more than 20 teams to prepare plans that would enable a smooth reentry.

Of all the plans that were developed, the COVID-19 virus testing presented the greatest challenge. The university considered hiring an outside firm to create and operate the program, but the cost was prohibitive, and reports from other institutions that had chosen to outsource were mixed. Hunter recognized the need to pivot to develop and implement the critically important COVID-19 testing program. Rapid deployment of the testing program was essential, so it was necessary to move ahead as soon as elements of the program were ready and to evolve the program over time. It required courage to move forward with so much uncertainty. Hunter shared[1]

> Our motto was "Start with YES." It was remarkable how much was accomplished simply because we believed in ourselves and one another. All team members were completely committed to the cause and were empowered to contribute in many ways. Although many of the members of the diverse team had never worked together previously, we developed tremendous trust and faith in one another's abilities early on. Team members were frank about their knowledge, skills, and abilities, which facilitated clear definition of roles and responsibilities. How-

---

[1]All quotations from Jane Hunter are from personal interviews with the authors, July 17, 2021.

ever, all the team members were extremely willing to learn and take on new challenges, so roles shifted rapidly as the team members grew.

The results of this optimistic vision quickly became apparent. The University of Arizona's COVID-19 testing program became a leading program, garnering attention across the nation. In September 2020, White House Coronavirus Task Force Leader Deborah Birx and her team visited the campus and noted that the Arizona testing method was a model for "transparently tracking COVID cases." In less than 2 months, the university provided over 33,000 COVID tests and reports on their COVID tracking portal. One can only imagine what would have happened if Hunter and her team had responded with "I'm not sure if we can do that" or "Well, that's really not what we do." With the optimistic vision and operationalized motto of "Start with YES," Hunter and her team not only bounced back in the wake of crisis but launched forward with innovation for the community.

Hunter is an excellent example of the first pillar of transformative resilient leadership: optimistic vision. Think about it: Who would you prefer to follow in a crisis with the goal of not just surviving, but thriving? Would it be a leader who is fearful, hesitant, and pessimistic? Would it be a leader who simply tries to minimize the losses associated with adversity? Or would it be a leader who is confident and has a vision for how to turn adversity into opportunity? Research and expert opinion suggest that people follow leaders with an optimistic vision, especially if they desire a better future (Everly et al., 2013, 2020; Goodwin, 2018).

OPTIMISTIC VISION DEFINED

Let's take a moment to define optimism as it applies here. *Optimism* is an attitude. It is the tendency to take the most positive or hopeful view of matters. It is the tendency to expect the best outcome, and it is the belief that good prevails over evil. Optimistic people are more persevering and resilient than pessimists, and they tend to be more task oriented and committed to success. Optimistic people tolerate adversity to a greater extent than do pessimists. They see adversity as temporary and well-circumscribed. The glass is always at least half full for the optimist, and that person will always have a reason to look forward to another day. The pessimist—not so much!

While an optimistic vision alone is not enough, and words must lead to actions in crisis, actions that are contextualized in an optimistic vision appear to be most readily embraced by those who follow. We refer to this characteristic as *active optimism,* and it is intended to foster resilience in those who follow.

Why is optimistic visionary leadership important for crisis leaders? Strategy formulation expert Nufer Yasin Ates conducts research and highlights the need for strategy alignment with leadership vision at all levels of business. He and his colleagues noted:

> Visionary leadership is widely seen as key to strategic change. That's because visionary leadership does not just set the strategic direction—it tells a story about *why* the change is worth pursuing and inspires people to embrace the change. Not surprisingly, then, science and practice have an incredibly positive view of visionary leadership as a critical leadership competency. (Ates et al., 2019)

In addition, it is likely that the active and consistent demonstration of such an attitude will prove contagious, helping to foster a *culture of resilience* as it serves as an active role model. And, when actively communicated, it can energize others. Active optimism is a way of harnessing expectation and turning it into the power of prophecy.

Are you an optimistic visionary leader? Complete the brief self-assessment in Table 5.1.

TABLE 5.1. Leadership Self-Assessment #1

Over the last month . . .	Seldom or never	Somewhat	Often	Almost always
1. I was confident in my ability to lead in adversity.	1	2	3	4
2. I demonstrated through my WORDS an optimistic vision for the future.	1	2	3	4
3. I was confident in my ability to use challenges and even failure as opportunities for growth.	1	2	3	4
4. I was confident in my ability to shape my own destiny and that of those around me.	1	2	3	4
5. I demonstrated through my ACTIONS an optimistic vision for the future.	1	2	3	4

Note. From the Resiliency Science Institutes, LLC, 2020. Reprinted with permission.

How did you do? The higher your score, the better. What are your strengths, and what areas could you improve in? I recommend using this survey periodically to assess your level of active optimism. The higher your score on the self-assessment survey, the greater your active optimism. Take your score and transfer it to the Five Pillars Summary Table in Appendix B. You will be able to record and track the degree of optimistic vision you experience month by month. Let's now take a closer look at both pessimism and optimism.

DID PESSIMISTIC LEADERSHIP CHANGE THE WORLD?

Pessimism is a losing strategy. Leadership requires both confidence and optimism in abundance.

—Toyotomi Hideyoshi,
16th-century Japanese warlord

Pessimistic leadership can have dire consequences. For example, at the beginning of World War II, Germany launched a surprise attack on France. The French were caught unprepared and began a retreat almost immediately. Although France and other Allied nations had important strategic advantages and could have fought back, French Prime Minister Paul Reynaud displayed pessimistic leadership when he resigned himself to defeat. Five days after the invasion began, Reynaud telephoned British Prime Minister Winston Churchill and said, "We have been defeated. We are beaten; we have lost the battle."

Churchill was a more optimistic visionary leader, and he argued that the battle was not lost, it was just beginning. In fact, the German tanks had exhausted their fuel. They had outrun their supply lines and were now sitting helplessly. This was a potentially catastrophic error by the German commanders. Churchill thought, given the strength of the Allies, surely a swift counterattack would be effective. But Reynaud refused Churchill's pleas. Eventually the German tanks refueled, and Germany succeeded in occupying France.

Like Churchill, some leaders see opportunity where others see only danger. The post–Civil War era was a time of great volatility and serial crises in America. Between 1868 and 1873, there was political turmoil, the collapse of gold prices and the ensuing public panic, the Great Chicago Fire, an equine influenza epidemic that left America without a means of local transportation, and the collapse of many financial markets. Southern "reconstruction" (rebuilding the Southern states after the American Civil War) came to a halt. The South fell deeper into economic despair. This was certainly no time to invest in the steel industry. But that's exactly what Andrew Carnegie did.

In 1848, at age 12, Carnegie arrived in the United States from Scotland. Though he began working as a telegrapher, by age 30, Carnegie had investments in railroads and oil derricks. As infrastructure investments were declining in 1870, he started construction of two blast furnaces for the manufacture of steel. Production began in 1872. He focused on mass producing inexpensive steel for the fabrication of rails for the railroad industry, which was crippled by the panic depression of 1873. Guided by an unflappable optimism, Carnegie boldly and persistently expanded his steel business into a vertically integrated empire until it became the largest steel company in the world and he became one of the richest men in the world.

Given that most people are pessimists burdened with a negativity bias, as we saw in Chapter 4, it is no wonder they seek to follow those rare individuals who possess a positive, optimistic outlook. It's more than the adage "opposites attract," rather people are drawn to those who can compensate for their own shortcomings. Winston Churchill and Andrew Carnegie were certainly examples of that type of compensatory leader: resilience-focused crisis leaders.

PASSIVE VERSUS ACTIVE OPTIMISM

Building a *culture of resilience* through effective leadership is not merely about avoiding pessimism and being optimistic, especially in crisis. Optimism itself has two vastly different forms. Optimism can be passive or active. If you are a passive optimist, it means that while you hope and believe things will turn out well in the future, you also believe that the future is in the hands of external forces. Believing that one's life largely resides outside of one's own control (dependent upon external forces, such as other people, luck, etc.) is known as having "an external locus of control" (Rotter, 1966). In contrast, active optimism means not only hoping and believing that the future will be positive but also believing in one's own ability to act to ensure the realization of desired goals. This belief in one's own power to effect change is referred to as an "internal locus of control" (Rotter, 1966). If you are an active optimist, then you have an internal locus of control, and you believe you can, within reason, shape your own destiny.

A related and critically important concept is self-efficacy, which was first defined by renowned psychologist Dr. Albert Bandura (1997). *Self-efficacy* is the belief in one's own ability to exercise control in a meaningful and positive way. More specifically, self-efficacy is the belief in one's ability to organize and execute the courses of action required to achieve necessary and desired goals. This perception of control, or influence, Bandura pointed out, is an essential aspect of life itself: "People guide their lives by their beliefs of personal efficacy" (p. 3). He went on to note that these beliefs in personal efficacy have far-reaching effects. Specifically, the beliefs influence the courses of action people take, their effort toward challenges, and how long they persist in the wake of hurdles or failures. If you possess high self-efficacy, it means you believe that you can act successfully as an agent of change acting on your own behalf or as a leader on the behalf of others when confronting uncertainty, adversity, crisis, or disaster. Thus, it is an actively optimistic and general expectation of success regardless of the adversity. Beliefs or self-appraisals of one's competence and ability to influence others will influence the behaviors, thoughts, and emotions of the leader and those who follow.

While the belief in one's own personal agency (self-efficacy) is critical, more recent evidence suggests that the belief that leaders have in their ability to create an environment wherein those who follow can be effective and accomplish collective goals is more important than the personal backgrounds or the personal beliefs that followers have in their own abilities (Donohoo, 2017; Hattie, 2016). This assertion of collective efficacy is critical for the crisis leader to understand and embrace. Thus, from our perspective, the purpose of active optimism and self-efficacy is not to predict the future, but to be an opportunity for the leader to create it. Active optimism is not a hope for the future, it is a mandate to change the future.

A FORMULA FOR BUILDING ACTIVE OPTIMISM WITHIN ASPIRING LEADERS

So, how can you use all this information to become a more effective leader? Bandura (1997) described four sources that affect the perception of self-efficacy and are particularly relevant in terms of the building of optimism and self-efficacy in aspiring leaders.

The most powerful way to increase self-efficacy and optimism is by experiencing success. Successes raise efficacy appraisals and optimism, while repeated failures lower efficacy appraisals and lead to pessimism. What is most amazing is that successful attainment is in the eye of the beholder. That is to say, objective success shows no favorable impact on self-efficacy or optimism if the individual *perceives* that success as "failure."

A second way to increase self-efficacy and optimism is through vicarious experiences. That is, if you watch someone like yourself succeed at something, you are more likely to be optimistic about your ability to succeed. If, on the other hand, you watch someone like yourself fail at something, you are more likely to be pessimistic about your ability to succeed:

> Self-efficacy appraisals are also partly influenced by vicarious experiences. Seeing or visualizing similar others perform successfully can raise self-percepts of efficacy in observers that they

too possess the capabilities to master comparable activities. . . . By the same token, observing others to be of similar competence fail despite high efforts lowers observer's judgments of their own capabilities and undermines their efforts. (Bandura, 1982, p. 27)

The most relevant and timely example of vicarious learning for leaders resides in observing how communities dealt with the COVID-19 pandemic. Communities that practiced lockdowns early, promoted tracing, vaccinations, physical distancing, and using masks experienced lower levels of infection. This was especially true during the Delta resurgence. Jacinda Ardern, prime minister of New Zealand, specifically cited how observations of the laxity of other countries had informed her bold decision to lockdown New Zealand after only a single case of the Delta variant emerged following 6 months of no cases at all.

Verbal encouragement and personal support are a third way to increase optimism and self-efficacy. Verbal encouragement included such things such as suggestion, education, and reinterpretation of experiences (e.g., finding opportunities to learn and iterate rather than failing). Finding an encouraging mentor or coach has long been known to enhance resilience as the connection, support, and challenge can be an antidote to lift someone through demanding situations. "Coaching" is an entire industry that arose over 20 years ago in recognition of the power of guidance from others. Reaching out and securing a mentor may be the most powerful option within this category. For over half a century I have seen and personally experienced the benefits of mentorship.

Finally, physical and emotional reactions may shape self-efficacy and even one's entire vision. As a result of his studies of self-efficacy and achievement, Bandura concluded that a single felt experience of arousal can facilitate or hinder performance. The perception of controlled exhilaration can improve self-efficacy, while the perception of uncontrolled arousal and stress can destroy self-efficacy in a heartbeat. Learning personal stress management techniques such as mindfulness and controlled breathing can aid in controlling adverse psychological reactions and fuel resilience. We recommend *A Clinical Guide to the Treatment of the Human Stress Response* (Everly & Lating, 2019). It is a classic, in print now for over 40 years.

HARNESSING THE POWER OF OPTIMISM: THE SELF-FULFILLING PROPHECY

> *Whether you think you can or you think you can't, you're right.*
> —Henry Ford

Active optimism has the potential to lead to a phenomenon known as the *self-fulfilling prophecy*, a term coined by sociologist Robert Merton in 1948. It is based on the *Thomas theorem*, which states that if we define situations as real, they become real in their consequences. If you expect failure, the likelihood of failure increases. If you expect success, the likelihood of success increases. But why? How does expectation become prophecy? If you think you will fail at something, you are likely to attempt the task with minimal effort, enthusiasm, and tenacity. You are more willing to accept initial rejection or failure. Or worse, you are likely not to attempt to be successful at all. On the other hand, if you think you will succeed at something, you are likely to attempt the task with greater effort, enthusiasm, and tenacity. You are less willing to accept initial rejection or failure. You are more likely to see those failures as exceptions to the rule and as simply precursors to the inevitable success. The self-fulfilling prophecy can be created from two perspectives: (a) self-created or (b) other-created (called the *Pygmalion effect*). The Pygmalion effect was identified by Rosenthal and Jacobsen (1968) when they observed that teacher expectations influence student performance. Indeed, if a teacher held positive expectations of students, they performed positively, while negative expectations influenced the students' performance negatively.

Expectation is a powerful force. Research going back over 40 years has shown that expectation can either increase or decrease the following: (a) the experience of pain, (b) blood flow to the brain and the stomach, (c) academic performance, (d) athletic performance, (e) panic attacks, (f) success in relationships (remember, confidence is a key variable in interpersonal attraction), (g) activity of the immune system (thus vulnerability to disease), and yes, (h) even the chance of sudden death (R. A. Jones, 1977). More important for the transformative leader, recent research and reviews have shown the Pygmalion effect as exerted by leaders to be a powerful determinant of the attitudes and successes of those who follow (Mo et al., 2021).

Individuals possessing a high sense of active optimism and self-efficacy (e.g., Churchill) are often task oriented and utilize multifaceted, integrative problem-solving skills to enhance successful outcomes when dealing with crises. Their preferred way of managing a crisis is to engage, communicate, and act boldly. As a result, they will exhibit high resilience in the wake of adversity. Conversely, people who exhibit pessimism with limited self-efficacy (e.g., Reynaud) may perceive crises as unmanageable and are more likely to dwell on perceived deficiencies, which generates increased stress and diminishes potential problem-solving energy, lowers aspirations, and weakens commitments. Their preferred way of managing a crisis is to retreat, avoid commitment, and hope to minimize losses. They tend to exhibit minimal resilience. Whether optimism or pessimism, whether self-created or other-created, such attitudes and self-fulfilling prophecies do affect others.

As noted earlier, in May 1940, the armies of Germany were engaged in the invasion of France. Due to the French withdrawal, fueled in part by Reynaud's defeatist attitude, they reached the French coast of the English Channel on May 20. Roughly 330,000 French, Belgian, and English soldiers became trapped around the French town of Dunkirk. Pushed up against the sea and surrounded by German forces, annihilation seemed inevitable. But on May 24, Adolf Hitler ordered his armies to halt their advance for 3 days. The reason for Hitler's hesitation remains unclear, but historians largely agree it was due to concerns over a potential British counterattack and the viability of the marshy terrain for a heavy armored assault. This hesitation gave the British precious time to plan and organize. On May 25, without meaningful consultation with the French, Churchill ordered the evacuation of all those trapped at Dunkirk. The British government put together the largest civilian armada in human history to sail to Dunkirk and rescue all those trapped from certain death or captivity. The rescue mission was not only successful in saving lives, but German General Von Rundstedt later called this campaign one of the turning points in the war. Other German generals felt the hesitation proved catastrophic.

BUILDING THE CULTURE OF RESILIENCY WITH ACTIVE OPTIMISM

So now the question arises: How can the transformative resilient leader build that culture of resilience using active optimism? What can one person do to change a culture? Malcom Gladwell, the journalist and bestselling author of *The Tipping Point* (2000), argued that a few strategically placed individuals can create a tipping point that can change a team, an organization, a community, even a country. We believe his assertion is noteworthy, but the question remains specifically as to how such cultural change can be achieved. The following recommendations are based on Bandura's (1997) self-efficacy framework.

First, understand that the culture of resilience begins at the top. Leaders should communicate their team's achievements to everyone in the organization, team, or community. More than anything else, communicating achievements reinforces the optimistic vision and expectation of future success. Leaders should emphasize the importance of successes no matter how small, while minimizing the importance of failures (i.e., seeing them as exceptions to the rule). Success builds collective efficacy.

The wise resilient crisis leader prepares for a crisis by ensuring their team has successes. Simply said, make your own self-fulfilling prophecy. Set your team up to succeed. Give them opportunities for success and mastery. When a challenge is large and overwhelming, break it down into smaller, more manageable parts. Approach those parts one at a time. The resilient leader would be wise to learn from the great Carthaginian general of the 3rd century B.C.E., Hannibal. Hannibal was remarkably successful in war by choosing the time and location of his battles. He was able to consistently defeat much larger armies by "choosing his battles" and "choosing the battlefield." He also chose to fight many smaller battles rather than one large battle, if possible. Armed with a vision, the self-fulfilling prophecy, and previous successes, when the unexpected crisis arises the team will be well prepared.

When team members lack the skill to have successes on their own, allow them to observe successes. Vicarious successful experiences fuel the vision and the self-fulfilling prophecy, as well. Clearly, one can learn how to be successful by studying both the successes and failures of others. The key is to keep the optimistic vision and the belief in the self-fulfilling prophecy alive.

While creating and communicating actual and vicarious success, it is imperative that the resilient leader repeatedly and consistently communicate the optimistic vision. Verbal persuasion and encouragement fuel the self-fulfilling prophecy. Parents, coaches, teachers, friends, and role models can impact the self-efficacy and collective efficacy of others by believing in the other person, the team, or organization and expressing that belief in supportive and encouraging ways.

U.S. Army Lieutenant General Hal Moore has frequently been described as one of the top generals/leaders in history. He is perhaps most famous for his command of the 1st Battalion of the 7th Cavalry Regiment during the war in Vietnam. In 1965, he was a lieutenant colonel, responsible for commanding and training over 400 inexperienced soldiers who would soon be deployed to war. As reported in *Armchair General* magazine, Moore understood that an optimistic vision matters. He understood that encouragement matters. During training, Moore told his inexperienced troops:

> We're a good Battalion, but we're gonna get a hell of a lot better. I will do my best and expect the same from each of you. We will be . . . without equal. We will be the best infantry Battalion in the world! Now go back to your barracks and get rid of all the 2nd place trophies. From now on, only 1st place trophies will be awarded, accepted or displayed in this outfit. In our line of work if we come in second, we are defeated on the battlefield. From now on, we are interested only in winning! We are without equal! (Moore, 2009)

In November 1965, he and his soldiers were indeed deployed to the jungles of Vietnam. There they participated in the first major battle of the war. Their unit was sent to reinforce a detachment of U.S. soldiers. Upon landing, they were quickly surrounded by more than 2,000 North Vietnamese troops near the Ia Drang Valley. Over the course of 3 days, Moore's forces defeated the North Vietnamese. His remarkable exploits were retold in the movie *We Were Soldiers* (Wallace, 2002).

PROFILES IN TRANSFORMATIVE RESILIENT LEADERSHIP:
Jon Luther, Iconic CEO

What do Popeye's, Dunkin' Donuts, and Arby's have in common? If you guessed that they are popular and phenomenally successful restaurant chains, you'd be correct. But what you probably don't know is that they all experienced dire financial crises. Last, you probably don't know that one man served as the primary architect for each of their transformations. His name is Jon Luther.[2]

Background

In the food service industry, Jon Luther is an icon. He's also a prime exemplar of what a transformative resilient leader would look like across all industries, not just the restaurant industry. His career is the story of a remarkable ability to rebound from crisis, reset direction, and accomplish extraordinary successes, not just once but time after time after time! Let's learn more about Jon and the key to his success. As Jon put it:

> Everyone is just a kid from somewhere. I was a kid from the Gibson Street Projects located along the Niagara River near Buffalo, NY. I found my way through college and finally graduated from a small school with a degree in hotel/restaurant management. I was married in my final semester of college. Our first child arrived 12 months later. I was 23 years old. I had no idea what life was going look like "down the road," and I should mention we were stone broke with an uncertain future!
>
> I started my career managing employee cafeterias, then moving into sales selling those services at Aramark. I spent 15 years at Aramark beginning as a salesperson selling vending

---

[2]All quotations from Jon Luther are from personal interviews with the authors, July 17, 2021.

88

services. I advanced to a senior role in marketing. And finally, to president of Aramark's luxury restaurant division.

So, one must pause here and ask, how did Jon go from vending sales to president of the luxury restaurant division? It seems like a unprecedented leap. Jon responded,

> This track record was accomplished because I would not allow my average education pedigree to define me. I simply worked harder to gain respect in all my career moves. I learned that I could compete rather well with the MBAs who wore their degree on their sleeve as opposed to rolling them up and learning how to lead and how to inspire their teams. Perhaps the most important lesson I learned was to anticipate how changes in direction, strategy, and policy affect those who must implement those changes. I learned in order for transformation to be successful, they must believe in my vision and my leadership finding them worthy and noble.

The Crisis/Challenge

Jon described his challenge as follows:

> After the luxury restaurant division was dissolved, I ventured out on my own for 10 years to find a new path. I had limited financial resources, but eventually partnered with a firm to acquire regional food service companies. After initial successes, the firm panicked and decided to end funding our initiatives. This meant terminating my employment. They actually came in the middle of the night to take back my company car without telling me. Imagine my surprise! I can smile today, but when it happened there was nothing funny about it. My dreams of success and security were devastated. No job, no severance, two kids in college, and did I mention, no car. You get the picture. I believe the saying is "bloodied, but

unbowed," I worked every day to try to find a sustainable future. Unwilling to bounce back to just any job that would simply stop the financial bleeding, I believed my next move needed to be a step up. I needed to spring forward. I know, sounds unrealistic. I had this persistent optimistic belief that something good would happen. Then it did.

Actions Taken/Lessons Learned

Jon's leadership is largely responsible for, not one nor two, but several of the most significant and impactful crisis transformations in his industry. Jon told us the stories of these crisis transformations with now iconic brands.

Birth of the Gateway Concept[SM]

His transformative resilient leadership consisted of having a powerful, optimistic vision even during what some saw as the worst of times:

> I was given the opportunity to become president of CA One Services, a subsidiary of Delaware North. CA One managed the food concessions, bars, and restaurants at 38 airports around the U.S. with over 300 locations. The business was a classic turnaround. The business was debt ladened, with high rents, tired facilities, poor quality products, and high prices (in fact, we joked that folks would come into our bar locations to sober up, they were so unappealing). I inherited a team that was mired in the status quo, standing still, not recognizing that the entity was in crisis. They had lost their strategic vision and had a hard time seeing a new one. But Jerry Jacobs, its chairman and Richards Stephens, its CEO, assured me they would support the changes needed. That support enabled me to transform CA One into an industry leading entity by adapting a radical innovation: The Gateway Concept.

The concepts were simple. We would start by upgrading our facilities. Next, we would implement our Gateway Concept. I saw airports as not only travel gateways, but food and beverage gateways as well. I convinced famous brands to join us. We ultimately partnered with Chef Wolfgang Puck, El Charro, Disney, Jack Nicklaus, Chef Masaharu Morimoto, The Food Network, and Jay-Z, just to name a few, to bring the most beloved food and beverages of the region into their airports. The results were impressive. From crisis, we saw a major transformation. We saw increased profitability. Our brand image was not only restored, but it was also greatly enhanced. The team members were proud to be winners!! It was a turnaround in my career, as well.

Be Good Bayou—Cajun Our Way

It's been said success begets success. That was true for Jon. As a result of his success with the transformational Gateway Concept, he was recruited to Popeyes as its president. The Popeyes chain of restaurants was in desperate need of transformative resilient leadership, as it was in bankruptcy with franchisees in disarray lacking guidance. Jon described the situation as another "classic turnaround opportunity":

> We took the brand back to its New Orleans/Southern Louisiana roots, expanding the menu beyond fried chicken and establishing a strategic heartbeat of "Cajun Our Way." We promised consumers that the food would "Be Good Bayou." Again, not without significant challenges. Franchisees had difficulty accepting a new strategic vision. Franchisees resisted "Cajun our Way," they said, "No way." We transformed our image, changing the look of our restaurants to reflect the Cajun Louisiana image. We launched "Louisiana Legends" shifting more to seafood and partnering with popular New Orleans chefs, Paul Prudomme, John Folse, Leah Chase, to develop new menu enhancements. "Louisiana Legends" won a Menu Masters award. Our menu

expansion and new facility look fostered amazing results, nearly doubling the number of stores. Annual unit volume became the highest in our industry category.

The Birth of "America Runs on Dunkin'"

As noted earlier, success often leads to further success. Jon had become the preeminent transformative crisis leader (turnaround guru) in his industry. But more challenges awaited him. Jon was recruited to become chairman/CEO at Dunkin' Brands (Dunkin' Donuts and Baskin Robbins). He described a new challenge:

> Dunkin' was a regional donut chain centered in New England. Donuts were their strategic focus. However, over 50% of store sales were coffee or related items. We were actually coffee shops disguised as donut shops. Once again, the management team was set firmly where they were in the marketplace . . . not on where they could be! Standing still, they were afraid to set a bold path and adopt a transformative strategic vision.
>
> I rebuilt the team using a vision and a values-based leadership approach, driving those values in our system to build trust. Our core leadership values were: (1) Honesty—you can always recover from the truth; (2) Integrity—character shows when no one is looking; (3) Fair but firm—use a disciplined approach; (4) Give people their dignity—no matter who they are; (5) Earn respect by actions—never demand or use position for personal benefit; and (6) Do the right thing—Always!!
>
> We refocused the brand with the tagline "America Runs on Dunkin'" and focused on coffee and breakfast. We changed cooking platforms to enhance speed of service and deliver product quality. We restructured the menu with award-winning new items. Once proven, I asked the team to follow me as we "crossed the Hudson" into new geographic markets! Shortly thereafter, we grew the store base of 4,000 stores to 7,500.

92

Both franchisee and brand profits experienced major increases. We acquired the company from parent and then took it public several years later. Today Dunkin' is an iconic brand and one of top 10 restaurant brands in the world.

Arby's: "We Have the Meats"

And then came Arby's. By now you know the story. Jon described the brand as "badly managed" and having lost its strategic vision:

As chairman, I began to initiate the change required to breathe new life into this brand. In the midst of the crisis, we transformed strategically. We sought to reinspire franchisees. No longer would we be considered a roast beef brand. Moving forward we would be a high-quality sandwich brand . . . "We Have the Meats." We created the promise of "Deli-Inspired" sandwiches, created Smokehouse Brisket, Gyro's, high-quality fish [Ocean Meat], and added "better for you" Market Fresh sandwiches, such as Pecan Chicken Salad. Quality improvements, better marketing, new menu items led to greater profits enabling reinvestment in stores, The results? Not just bouncing back, but a transformational turnaround . . . profits increased tenfold! From this beginning, I recruited a first-class CEO who continued its progress acquiring several new brands [including Dunkin'] . . . now Inspire Brands . . . one of the top five restaurant enterprises in the world.

Profile Summary

We began this profile by saying Jon Luther is an icon in his industry. He's also a prime exemplar of what a transformative resilient leader would look like across all industries. What are the major lessons to be learned? The power of tenacity, the necessity of a moral compass, and the most important theme that emerges from each of the transformations described above: the importance of an optimistic, motivating strategic vision. Organizations in crisis often suffer from a lack of strategic vision suited to the time and marketplace. Personally, Jon likes to quote Gandhi (1920), who said, "Strength does not come from physical capacity. It comes from an indomitable will." For the transformative resilient leader that seems a sine qua non and is personified in Jon Luther: a humble and congenial man with uncanny prescient vision, who practices our covenant of strength and honor with an indomitable will.

KEY POINT SUMMARY

- The transformative resilient leader knows that to be sustained, transformative resilience must not rest solely on the shoulders of the leader; rather, sustainable opportunity-focused change must reside within a culture of resilience.
- One powerful way of building that culture of resilience is through a vision constructed from active optimism and the self-fulfilling prophecy, especially the Pygmalion effect.
- A self-fulfilling prophecy is a prediction that comes true because someone believes the prediction. When we believe something will happen, we act in ways that fulfill the belief.
- Optimism is the tendency to take the most positive or hopeful view of matters. In the context of transformative resilient leadership, optimism is the ability to personally lead with an optimistic vision, to see opportunity where others see adversity, as well as to model and communicate optimism for others, especially in crisis, and then weave that into the cultural fabric of the organization or community.
- Success breeds success. The most powerful way to increase optimism is to experience success because it increases our sense of self-efficacy and leads to self-fulfilling prophecies. Thus, optimistic leaders communicate and celebrate successes with their teams.

- Leaders such as Dr. Jane Hunter and Jon Luther are the embodiment of transformative resilient leadership, as they each used a compelling optimistic vision to overcome inertia and motivate transformational change. Hunter led and navigated a historical threat to the university community with innovation and national-leading solutions. Luther not only employed vision-motivated change to enhance profitability for several now iconic brands, but he has used it to change an entire industry.

CHAPTER 6

DECISIVENESS

We are taught to understand, correctly, that courage is not the absence of fear, but the capacity for action despite our fears.
—John McCain

On November 17, 2019, cases of an unusual pneumonia were first observed in the city of Wuhan, China. On December 31, 2019, health officials in China reported 41 such cases to the World Health Organization (WHO). On January 7, 2020, the pathogenic agent was identified as a novel coronavirus, later named COVID-19 by WHO. The virus spread rapidly outside of Wuhan. On January 13, 2020, the first case of the virus outside of China was reported in the country of Thailand. On January 30, 2020, WHO declared a Public Health Emergency of International Concern, and officially declared it a pandemic on March 11, 2020.

As we look at the COVID-19 pandemic, it has been challenging to find examples of effective crisis leadership, especially transformative resilient leadership, at the governmental level. Yet, according to the *Bloomberg Resilience Ranking* (Bloomberg News, 2021), New Zealand was ranked #1 in resilience scores when assessing the world for its COVID response after year one. The key to New Zealand's success was immediate truthful and transparent communication from the Ministry of Health, decisive action without hesitation from the Prime Minister, and early and stringent intervention. Specifically:

- On February 3, 2020, the Prime Minister of New Zealand Jacinda Ardern banned entry to any foreigner coming from China. Any New Zealander returning from China was compelled to go into isolation for 14 days.
- On February 28, 2020, the first case of COVID-19 was confirmed by the Ministry of Health in New Zealand and on March 19, Ardern closed New Zealand's borders to all noncitizens and nonresidents. Ardern addressed her nation, saying these were the most severe restrictions anywhere in the world, and for which she would "make no apologies." But she would implement even greater restrictions.
- On March 25, after only 283 confirmed cases, Ardern announced the implementation of a four-level national alert system—which would give people a clear means of tracking the evolving situation—and declared a national state of emergency.
- On March 26, a national lockdown and self-isolation were instituted.

A lockdown on international travel coupled with guidance on domestic isolation and contact tracing at the earliest stages of viral impact resulted in a rapid decline in the transmission of the virus. "The lockdown implemented in New Zealand was remarkable for its stringency and its brevity" (Robert, 2020, p. E569). Professor Michael Baker, a top epidemiologist with the New Zealand Department of Health, indicated,

> officials did an "absolutely remarkable job" of implementing New Zealand's lockdown. Even at its peak, New Zealand had only 89 cases a day. "They really engaged the minds and hearts

of the population into doing the unthinkable, of saying go home and stay there for the best part of six weeks." (A. Jones, 2020)

Amid the Delta variant resurgence in mid-August 2021, even after 6 weeks of no COVID-19 cases, Ardern once again decisively locked down her country. The precipitating event was a single COVID-19 case. Ardern's actions were not only exemplary of effective crisis leadership, but they were also exemplary of growth promoting transformative resilient leadership. The *Bloomberg Media Survey* (Farrer, 2020) of over 700 senior business executives rated the country of New Zealand, under the leadership of Prime Minister Jacinda Ardern, as having the most effective crisis response to the COVID-19 pandemic of any country in the world. Her leadership garnered for New Zealand recognition as the country in which respondents would have the greatest confidence to invest. The benefit of foreign investment is obvious. Not only would it foster economic resilience in the wake of the pandemic, but it would build a stronger economic infrastructure for future economic prosperity.

In contrast to the decisive leadership in New Zealand, consider the indecisiveness of the United States during this same period. In the aforementioned publication, *The Bloomberg Resilience Ranking* (Bloomberg News, 2021), the United States received a resilience score hovering around 60, ranked #21 at the end of the first quarter of 2021. While Chapter 5 described one leader's success in addressing the COVID-19 pandemic at a university, U.S. government leaders failed to provide such leadership during the crisis. An article in *Scientific American* (Lewis, 2021b) noted national elected officials' and public health officials' indecision plagued the public health response to COVID-19 and undoubtedly resulted in more deaths than might otherwise have otherwise occurred: (a) initially, the Centers for Disease Control and Prevention (CDC) and other U.S.

government sources downplayed the severity of the virus; (b) the U.S. government was slow to approve COVID detection tests made by private companies or in other countries, choosing instead to develop its own; (c) in addition to being flawed, U.S. sources could not manufacture the tests fast enough to keep up with demand; (d) CDC initially dissuaded people from buying and using masks, later changing its position on their importance; and (e) the lack of centralized decision making regarding physical distancing, quarantine, and vaccination from federal government sources relegated most of the COVID public health response to individual states, resulting in highly varied response measures. Vaccination appeared an effective deterrent to the continued spread of the COVID-19 virus, but only about 50% of the U.S. population was fully vaccinated as COVID approached its third winter. Clearly, personal indecision played a role in lower than desirable rates on vaccination.

In this chapter, we focus on the art of decision making, as it is the launching pad for the self-fulfilling prophecy discussed in the previous chapter. Listed below is Leadership Self-Assessment #2 in Table 6.1. Please complete the self-assessment and score it. The higher your score, the more decisive you are. Transfer your score to the tracking tool at the end of the book.

With improved leadership decisiveness in mind, let's take a closer look at barriers to effective decision making in crisis: (a) hesitation; (b) oversimplification; (c) the failure to understand the unintended consequences of one's decisions; and (d) impulsive actions and how to move past such inclinations.

BARRIERS TO EFFECTIVE DECISION MAKING

Several barriers stand between leaders and their ability to make their best decisions. Transformative resilient leaders need to understand these barriers in order to overcome them.

Over the last month . . .	Seldom or never	Somewhat	Often	Almost always
6. Based on my WORDS, people would consider me a decisive person.	1	2	3	4
7. I considered both the short- and long-term impact of my decisions.	1	2	3	4
8. Based on my ACTIONS, people would consider me a decisive person.	1	2	3	4
9. I consistently sought opportunity in challenge or adversity.	1	2	3	4
10. If change was necessary, I did not hesitate.	1	2	3	4

TABLE 6.1. Leadership Self-Assessment #2

Note. From the Resiliency Science Institutes, LLC, 2020. Reprinted with permission.

Moving Past Hesitation

> *The way to develop decisiveness is to start right where you are, with the very next question you face.*
>
> —Napoleon Hill

Transformative resilient leaders should understand that the first barrier to their own decision making (as well as whether those who follow choose to follow leadership guidance) is hesitation. It is common to hesitate before deciding. Analysis in the service of error avoidance is laudable. That said, *paralysis by analysis* can be catastrophic, as was demonstrated to some degree during the COVID-19 pandemic. The previous section raised the question of whether such a paralytic response might have changed the outcome of a world war. The same question may be asked about the pandemic. Physiologists have long known that the human stress response has three aspects to it: fight, retreat, or paralysis. In such a context, we think of the stress response as the "fight, flight, or freeze" response. Hesitation can be dangerous in life-threatening situations. Paralysis by analysis can not only be costly in international affairs, it can also contribute to economic catastrophe, as was the case when Herbert Hoover's indecision regarding reform of a failing banking system led to the crash of 1929, which launched the Great Depression. How can we reduce the likelihood of costly hesitation and perhaps even complete paralysis in crisis decision making?

To remedy hesitation, we must first understand its main cause, which is uncertainty, that is, the inability to understand the link between action or inaction, on one hand, with their consequences on the other hand. Blaise Pascal was a 17th-century French polymath. He is credited with being one of the first inventors of the mechanical calculator, called the *Pascaline*. From mathematician, he morphed into philosopher, and finally theologian. His most famous theological work was entitled *Pensees* (Thoughts), which was considered a classic. In his contemplations of the existence of God, Pascal offered insight into fundamental decision making that is applicable in all situations. The paradigm is referred to as *Pascal's wager*. The paradigm is a simple cost–benefit analysis that helps link actions with consequences while revealing potentially unintended consequences. It can be applied to any decision you will ever make. It helps us move past hesitation by giving us definable options and likely outcome.

To use Pascal's wager, simply propose an action or solution to a problem and answer the following four questions:

1. What is the best likely outcome that can be achieved if I act?
2. What is the best likely outcome that can be achieved if I do not act?
3. What is the worst likely outcome if I act?
4. What is the worst likely outcome if I do not act?

We sought an example of Pascal's wager far removed from theology. So, we investigated high-risk surgical decision making. The Johns Hopkins surgeon Dr. Ben Carson was perhaps one of the greatest neurosurgeons of his era. He successfully performed surgeries at which others had failed. He successfully performed surgeries no one else had even attempted. When we asked him how he decided whether to perform a high-risk surgery or not, he responded with a variation of Pascal's wager by asking himself the following four questions:

1. What is the best outcome that can be achieved if I perform the surgery?
2. What is the best outcome that can be achieved if I do not perform the surgery?
3. What is the worst outcome if I perform the surgery?
4. What is the worst outcome if I do not perform the surgery?

So, what's the remedy to hesitation? Asking yourself these four questions prior to making a decision simplifies what might seem like an overwhelming challenge in decision making. Pascal's wager provides us with greater insight into the ramifications of our decisions, creates a feeling of greater control, and helps us move past hesitation with greater confidence by making the analytic process finite rather than infinite and thus paralyzing.

In Crisis, the Brain Creates Error-Prone Oversimplifications

Although it is important not to get overwhelmed by consideration factors, it is also important not to oversimplify the issues. Our second barrier to effective decision making in crisis is our tendency to take oversimplifying shortcuts. In crisis, the brain is bombarded with information. To manage all these data, the brain creates information-processing shortcuts, or *simplifications*. An information-processing simplification (sometimes called bias) is a processing filter that often results from being confronted with incomplete or overwhelming amounts of information. Simplifications streamline or attempt to clarify large or incomplete data sets and allow us to reach decisions that would otherwise be daunting. They also conserve precious mental energy in that they require relatively low amounts of brain glucose. As such, these simplifications are "default programs" especially in stressful situations. These simplifications do indeed simplify decision making more important however, they often lead us to make mistakes. Some oversimplifications are related to the System 1 intuitive thought processes we reviewed in Chapter 4, but we expand upon that notion here to underscore their effects upon resilience-focused decision making.

Five Common Biases

It has been said that recognition is the first step toward solving a problem. So, what do these error-prone shortcuts look like? Here are five common biases and remedial suggestions.

Dunning–Kruger Effect

Have you ever met a person who consistently thought they were more competent than they actually were? They embody a general sense of overconfidence or overestimate their knowledge, skills, and abilities to execute effectively. This is a form of cognitive bias. It can be especially problematic when found in managers and leaders of any type. This bias is referred to as the *Dunning–Kruger effect* (Kruger & Dunning, 1999). Some refer to it as "ignorance of one's own ignorance." It's also referred to as metaignorance, which simply refers to the inability to step back and see one's own actions objectively. While problematic in everyday leadership, it can be catastrophic in crisis. Leadership errors in crisis are the errors most likely to have the greatest negative impact on followers and the organization as a whole.

Dunning–Kruger remedies are essential for any leader. To combat this risk, leaders are advised to first slow down in their decision making. As with any biases, the Dunning–Kruger effect is tempered with an opportunity to reflect on the influences on the situation, including the internal processes. During this time, leaders may intentionally consider counterarguments to their beliefs or decisional paths. Consider acting as an internal "devil's advocate." Further, leaders who are cognitively flexible and willing to take criticism as data for growth rather than becoming rigid in "knowing" can mitigate the risk that they are developing an inflated sense of competence.

BINARY THINKING

When confronted with ambiguous or an overwhelming amount of data, we tend to boil decisions down to simple "all or none," "yes or no" decisions. However, the world we live in is dimensional, not binary. Binary decision making increases volatility. It causes us to ignore the details that can be the difference between success and failure.

To remedy binary thinking, the leader must analyze the validity of all-or-none binary thinking. Very few things in life are all-or-none decisions. Rather, solutions are more attainable if we view situations dimensionally. Through the adoption of dimensional thinking, risk can often be reduced and compromise attained.

BIAS-CONFIRMATIVE THINKING

The brain does not like dissonance. As a result, it searches for information that confirms the biases we already hold and the decisions we've already made. It rejects anything that does not fit our pre-determined narrative. This simplification makes compromise with others impossible. It hinders creativity. It foretells the demise of the organization or system within which it becomes the norm.

To remedy bias-confirmative thinking, the leader should always encourage a *devil's advocate* perspective as a means of countering the potential for confirmatory bias. Rather than focus on information that supports your foredrawn or most preferred conclusions, focus on any anomaly that might contradict your conclusions. Similarly, when faced with the problem of conflicting evidence, rather than decide by accepting the majority of evidence at face value, focus on the anomaly, a piece of evidence that doesn't fit, until you are convinced it is either invalid or actually provides the greatest insight of all. Keep in mind the admonition "Know or know not, there is no I assume."

SHORT-TERM EFFECT THINKING

This refers to our short-sighted tendency to make decisions thinking only of the primary short-term outcome desired. This is especially relevant in the acute "fog of crisis" where acute survival may become the only priority. While focus on acute survival is of course essential, such exclusive focus prohibits us from considering the intermediate and long-term consequences of our decisions.

To remedy short-term effect thinking, the leader should consider the intermediate and long-term effect of your decisions. This will help protect against unanticipated consequences. A common prompt is the 10–10–10 question: What will be the impact of this choice in 10 minutes? 10 weeks? 10 months? Others have modified it to considering 10 years based on the nature of the crisis. Regardless, find a go-to query that can help pull you from a narrowed fog of immediacy.

LEGACY-EFFECT THINKING

Some leaders become consumed with their "legacy." Legacy-effect thinking can be fueled by two distinct motivations: the admirable other-centric desire not to burden successors and future generations with the consequences of one's decisions, and the self-centric desire to ensure one's own place in history. Every decision exerts an unintended ripple effect, even the decision not to decide. History is replete with examples of problems made worse by the unintended consequences of their intended solutions. We review several in the next section.

To remedy legacy-effect thinking, leaders must understand that their desire to preserve the future may sacrifice the morale, dedication, and even productivity of their followers in the present. This, in and of itself, can adversely affect legacy. The self-centric legacy-focused leader must understand that their legacy will be tarnished in the long run by selfishness.

Law of Unintended Consequences

> *There are downsides to everything; there are unintended consequences to everything. The most corrosive piece of technology that I've ever seen is called television—but then, again, television, at its best, is magnificent.*
> —Steve Jobs

Our third barrier to effective decision making in crisis is the *law of unintended consequences* (LUC), which states that every action leads irrefutably to unforeseen and unintended consequences. Historian Daniel Boorstin has been credited with saying, "The unintended consequences of man's enterprises have and will always be more potent, more widespread, and more influential than those he intended" (Sherden, 2011, p. 1).

In 1936, Robert Merton published an important paper that is especially relevant to decision making during crisis. The paper is titled "The Unanticipated Consequences of Purposive Social Action" and was published in the prestigious journal *American Sociological Review*. He noted:

> In some of its numerous forms, the problem of the unanticipated consequences of purposive action has been treated by virtually every substantial contributor to the long history of social thought. The diversity of context and variety of terms by which this problem has been known, however, have tended to obscure the definite continuity in its consideration. (p. 894)

Unexpected consequences fall into three categories: (a) unexpected adverse outcomes, (b) unexpected positive outcomes, and (c) contrary effects wherein the opposite of the expected outcome occurs. Examples of LUC are legion. Here are a few:

- The term "cobra effect" refers to the colonial British government's (possibly apocryphal) attempt to reduce the number of cobras in Delhi by offering a bounty for every dead cobra. People began to breed cobras for the income. When the government became aware of this, the reward program was stopped, causing the cobra breeders to set the snakes free. As a result, the wild cobra population further increased. The apparent solution for the problem made the situation even worse.
- To speed up transit times, airlines restricted carry-on baggage size but allowed free check-in at the gate. This was designed to

speed up boarding time, as passengers did not have to struggle to find space in overhead bins and avoided delayed checking of bags. Unfortunately, this increased the number of gate checks, which actually delayed flight departures.

- In the 1980s, America witnessed a new war. This war was not about land, politics, or wealth. It was about soft drinks. The war has been referred to as the Cola Wars. It was fought between Pepsi-Cola and Coca-Cola. An aggressive marketing campaign mounted by Pepsi showed people in blind taste tests preferring the taste of Pepsi over Coke. Even though Coke remained the best-selling cola, it decided to change its flavor. On April 23, 1985, the chairman and CEO of Coca-Cola, Roberto Goizueta, introduced a new formula for Coca-Cola called New Coke. So confident was Goizueta, he stated, "Some may choose to call this the boldest single marketing move in the history of the packaged-goods business . . . we simply call it the surest move ever made." Corporate president Donald Keough proclaimed, "I've never been as confident about a decision as I am about the one we're announcing today." Within days, sales of Coca-Cola declined, demonstrators poured Coke into the streets, and the company's stock dropped on the New York Stock Exchange. Recognizing they had made the greatest blunder in the history of the packaged-goods business, on July 11, 1985, Coke announced it was bringing back the original formula Coke, now called Coca-Cola Classic. Even though blind taste tests performed by Coca-Cola showed that consumers actually preferred the new formula, corporate leaders at Coke failed to understand the adverse impact a change in formula would have on tradition and brand loyalty.
- And let us not forget about politicians who, with the best of intentions, promise to give their constituents benefits without planning for the often-adverse consequences of such increased

benefits and services, for example, deficit spending, higher taxes, delays in availability of accessing services, and creation of inefficient and wasteful bureaucracies to manage such benefits.

What are the major contributors to making decisions while failing to consider LUC? Merton (1936) described several factors that contribute to adverse unintended consequences: (a) acting without sufficient information; (b) viewing potential outcome as it affects oneself, rather than others; (c) fear of failure; and (d) acting on the basis of urgency, not importance—Merton referred to this as "imperious immediacy."

So, how can we reduce the risk of adverse consequences associated with LUC? Three overarching strategies may be of assistance:

1. Use Pascal's wager. This model of decision making serves to help us better understand our decision-making options and their consequences. Uncertainty fuels paralysis by analysis. Pascal's wager helps resolve uncertainty.
2. Focus on avoiding the confirmatory bias effect. Don't search for confirmation of your foredrawn conclusions, rather search for anomalous evidence.
3. Avoid "imperious urgency" by triaging demands on your time. Merton reminds us of the dangers of making decisions based on imperious urgency rather than overall importance. Unfortunately, one of the hallmark characteristics of crisis is time urgency. Time urgency can interfere with effective decision making. A simple crisis-oriented time management system that helps you triage demands can be very helpful in reducing this risk.

The term *triage* is of French origin and means to prioritize. The crisis leader is often confronted with myriad demands, many competing. Time and attention are limited commodities. Attempting to address all demands is a fool's errand, as it leads to fatigue. Fatigue leads to mistakes. Effective time management is essential. This begins by triaging demands.

Alan Lakein (1973) wrote an influential book on time management, *How to Get Control of Your Time and Your Life*. It has relevance for resilience-focused crisis leadership. Lakein noted that the demands upon our time come in three categories—Categories A, B, and C, where

A = Important and Urgent
B = Important not Urgent, or Urgent not Important
C = Neither Important, nor Urgent

Lakein (1973) argued that we are fooled into wasting precious time, energy, and resources by the characteristic urgency or importance of B demands. Feelings of frustration, bewilderment, and ultimately fatigue, with its consequential tendencies for mistakes, arise from attending to B demands. Why? B demands, Lakein argued, are demands in transition. Most B demands become C demands, neither urgent nor important. So, Lakein wrote, we should attend only to the A demands. Yes, some B demands will become A demands. When they do, address them. So what should crisis leaders do? Directly attend to A demands, make sure B demands are monitored, address C demands only when the crisis has passed, if at all.

Inclinations to Act Impulsively

Our fourth barrier to effective crisis decision making is to act impulsively, without much regard for rational cognitive input. In most cases, impulsive actions are based on faulty thinking processes. It will be recalled from Chapter 4, there are two very different styles of thinking: (a) reflexive, intuitive cognition (System 1) and (b) logical, rational cognition (System 2). System 1 thinks associatively, but it has little understanding of logic and probability, and frequently makes mistakes in judgment about these. Here we review and extend that discussion.

System 1 encourages us to be overconfident in what we think we know, and it fails to acknowledge the full extent of our ignorance. Its greatest weaknesses are that it is reflexive, is based on previous pattern recognition (biases), and fails to understand the consequences of actions, especially unintended consequences. It frequently leads to impulsive actions that are can be very wrong and sometimes catastrophic. So be wary of the encouragement to "always trust your gut." One further limitation of System 1 is that it cannot be turned off, only overridden!

System 2, on the other hand, thinks deterministically. It has an understanding of logic, cause and effect, and probability. System 2 can be cautious and can differentiate what we know from what we believe, absent evidence. If given time and effort, it can solve complex problems and lead to innovation. Its greatest weaknesses are that it requires effort and high amounts of glucose (energy). It is easily disrupted by stress and fatigue. One further limitation of System 2 is it is often overridden by System 1 decisions in high stress situations.

To reduce impulsivity, leaders should practice and model the following:

1. Deliberately practice being mindful. Be focused in the moment. Focus only upon that which is most important. Do not allow yourself to be distracted by noise, chaos, a flood of information, or competing demands.
2. When possible, delay making important decisions to a less stressful moment.
3. Take a couple of deep breaths. This tends to decelerate a racing heart, which is correlated with System 1 cognition.

4. Seek a dispassionate outside opinion.
5. Think what the unintended consequences of actions might be.
6. Assess the risk versus reward of actions, especially considering potential unintended consequences as the actions you take may have indirect, latent, and unintended consequences that can create problems larger than the problems your actions are intended to solve.

THE CHALLENGER DISASTER: A CASE OF FAILED DECISION MAKING

On January 28, 1986:

> Exactly 73.621 seconds after liftoff at 11:39 a.m., the space shuttle Challenger exploded, killing all seven persons on board. With the destruction of Challenger, America's dream for a quick and easy conquest of outer space died. A more obvious casualty of the Challenger disaster . . . the reputation of the National Aeronautics and Space Administration (NASA) was severely tarnished. The "can-do" attitude of NASA . . . was replaced by "can-fail" realism. NASA's aura of invincible professionalism was suddenly replaced with an image of bureaucratic bungling and institutional fallibility. (Harrison, 1993, p. 161)

The presidential commission to investigate the disaster (Rogers Commission) concluded that NASA's decision to launch Challenger was flawed. NASA decision makers fell prey to at least the problems enumerated above: (a) they disregarded the risks and LUC (worst case if we launch); (b) they proceeded with the decision according to their own preference for timely launch, losing sight of the more important goal of progressing safe human space flight; (c) they ignored previous contractor admonitions (anomalies) against launch after cold weather that were at odds with their preferred outcome of launch; and (d) they fell prey to imperious urgency (United States, 1986).

PROFILES IN TRANSFORMATIVE RESILIENT LEADERSHIP:
Marco Sala, CEO of International Game Technology

When COVID-19 hit, international companies needed to adapt to changing conditions while keeping an eye on the future. Transformative resilient leaders like Marco Sala made this possible in very uncertain times.

Background

Marco Sala is CEO of International Game Technology (IGT) and serves on its board of directors. He is responsible for overseeing the strategic direction of IGT. In addition, Marco serves on the board of directors of IGT's parent company De Agostini S.p.A., a family-owned Italian holding company that directs strategic operations for IGT and other companies. Marco was educated in Milan, majoring in business and economics.

IGT is *the* global leader in gaming. It achieved its position of pre-eminence within its industry by designing, developing, manufacturing, and distributing high quality consumer-focused computerized game content, gaming equipment, software, and network systems. The company's products consist of turnkey lottery systems that enjoy a dominant worldwide market share as well as slot machines (such as the popular Wheel of Fortune slot machine), social gaming platforms, and other interactive gaming machines. With over 11,000 employees worldwide, the company has strategically crafted and maintains well-established local presences in more than 100 countries. IGT maintains the leading competitive positions across the global lottery and gaming marketplace. Revenues averaged $4.8 billion prior to the pandemic of 2020–2021.

The Crisis/Challenge

The COVID-19 pandemic proved devastating to many industries. While online gaming activities actually increased, the pandemic forced the shutdown of casinos and most related services worldwide. Alternatively, state-sponsored lotteries, by and large, remained operational and (but most important) required ongoing service. As the world's leading gaming operator, IGT maintains a significant presence not only in North America but in Italy and in China. In doing so, IGT was confronted with the adverse impacts of the COVID-19 virus in the earliest stages of the pandemic's spread. Sala[1] notes, "IGT operations in Italy, a significant financial contributor, were closing and IGT's development center in China were adversely impacted well before others." The gaming capital of the world is the Chinese special administrative region of Macau. It generates almost 5 times the gaming revenue of Las Vegas. Initially, all of this virtually came to a halt. American commercial gaming income alone declined by roughly 31% in 2020.

Actions Taken/Lessons Learned

Marco Sala and his colleagues understood the urgency of the crisis and acted accordingly. He noted:

> In March of 2020, many things were unknown about COVID-19, but it was clear that fundamental and urgent actions would be required to guarantee the viability of IGT's business in the face of the pandemic. A COVID-19 Crisis Management Committee, with the senior leadership team at its core, was quickly configured.

The goal of the committee was to act both tactically and strategically. Tactically, its job was to identify and prioritize immediate actions necessary to ensure employee and customer protection, business continuity, and cash preservation. At the same time, it had to act strategically. Its job was to formulate and implement initiatives that would streamline the organizational structure, reconfigure supply chains, reduce costs, and provide tangible reassurance to the board of directors and investors, alike.

---

[1] All quotations from Marco Sala are from personal correspondence with the authors, May 4, 2021.

The overarching guidance to the crisis committee was straightforward—respond to what you know, adapt as that evolves, don't be distracted by the unknown, act decisively and quickly, keep stakeholders informed, be open and transparent, and ensure policies and solutions are equitable.

And how was the tactical guidance implemented?

Workstreams with senior manager leads were structured around employee and customer protection, scenario planning, capital expenditure optimization, cost-saving initiatives, improving working capital, and ensuring business continuity.

A stress case was developed to test the resiliency of the business. It also served as the basis of the approach made to IGT's lenders to renegotiate the company's entire portfolio of credit instruments to ensure long term availability of resources and to seek debt covenant relief. Existing liquidity appeared to be sufficient to weather the crisis. Nevertheless, the leadership team started managing the business to conserve cash and identify mitigating actions to reduce operational costs and capital expenditures. From the CEO on down, everyone would be asked to accept a reduced salary. Some furloughs would be necessary. Fairness and equitable treatment are part of IGT's core values. Clearly, these actions would define and drive IGT's culture and relationship with its workforce for years to come. It is important to note that the senior leadership team voluntarily accepted and endorsed this recommendation to the Board for adoption. The Board's appreciation of the commitment of IGT's leadership was an important factor in building confidence in the crisis plan.

Sala also emphasized the importance of communications:

For employees, a comprehensive communications plan was launched that featured easily accessed, centralized information.

Local managers were empowered to react to circumstances in their regions to determine the best application of corporate guidance. An open letter from the CEO to all employees was candid and direct. The company was absorbing substantial COVID-related impacts.

Sala explained how he and his team operationalized a strategic transformative approach to crisis leadership:

To begin, financially, there was a successful restructuring of IGT debt under favorable terms that provides for ample liquidity to cover debt maturities through 2022. Programs were identified for over $200 million in structural cost reductions.

A reorganization and simplification of the business model was launched in June 2020. Strategic initiatives already in planning were fast-tracked. The new organization is better able to capture growth.

The result was a remarkable year:

Impressively, there was a 50 percent growth in Digital & Betting service revenue in 2020, mostly led by an expanding player base in existing markets. Gaming is rebounding well. Most casinos in North America are open. The combination of strong Lottery performance and disciplined cost and capital management delivered the highest level of free cash flow generation in the last 5 years. IGT's performance far surpassed market expectations and has sustained and grown the confidence of the Board in the management team.

From a customer perspective, IGT's efforts to support them during the pandemic have fortified and strengthened our relationships for the long term.

During 2020, an employee survey was conducted. Despite having implemented furloughs, pay cuts, pandemic restrictions, and a major reorganization, the survey trends actually indicate significant improvements in the employee experience. The engagement index, which measures pride and commitment to the company, rose to 79% a 4.5% jump from our 2018 survey.

IGT responded to the COVID pandemic well. All in all, momentum has been created that will continue throughout 2021 and that bodes well for the future of IGT. There are important takeaways from our experience:

1. Protecting employees is a first-line priority.
2. Overall, people will execute on a strategy, no matter how daunting the challenge, if they feel part of it, understand the path to success and know that their sacrifice is shared and appreciated.
3. Open honest communication is essential.
4. Equitable treatment is empowering. Sharing the sacrifices leads to a greater commitment by the workforce to the future of the company.
5. Addressing a crisis should not distract leaders from the important strategic initiatives that need to be undertaken to better guarantee the long-term health of the business. In other words, doing what's right for the business, even during times of crisis and disruption, must remain paramount. The structural reorganization of IGT is a prime example. It positioned the company for continued leadership in lottery and gaming and was undertaken as the pandemic closed or disrupted our markets around the world. It was a challenge to institute. Crafting new financial reporting schemes and organizational structures taxed the capacity of our teams but they delivered. Delaying implementation, an obvious option, would have been detrimental to the business and forestalled our long-term progress and vision.
6. Dealing with a crisis can make you stronger if you recognize and act on the opportunities it presents. It is important to have the crisis awaken the leadership to new realities. By focusing on priorities that are creating value and examining

processes for greater efficiencies, the company will emerge stronger. It is not unlike a zero-based budgeting exercise. For example, the Italian machine gaming market is being consolidated. That presented an opportunity to dispose of an asset whose contribution was under pressure. Similarly, IGT's supply chain model was outmoded. An outsourcing model was instituted that has greater efficiency and flexibility and an improved cost basis for our products. Manufacturing operations were significantly reduced at considerable savings that are structural in nature. Another example is travel. Travel has long been viewed as a necessity to maintain employee and customer relationships. The pandemic changed that overnight. Now, virtual technologies enable and drive our relationships eliminating expensive in-person visits. Savings in this area are significant and will become structural as a new approach has taken hold. The same is true for marketing. The gaming industry centers on major trade shows to highlight products and services. Due to the pandemic, the shows that require major investment by exhibitors, were canceled. Some version of the shows will return but new marketing initiatives that are much more cost-effective have been developed and customers are responding.

7. The point of these examples is that IGT is positioned for continued success not so much despite being dramatically impacted by the pandemic but because we were dramatically impacted by the pandemic. Our performance is upending assumptions about the capability of a gaming business to not only endure a pandemic but also take steps to better position itself for continued growth and leadership in the industry. IGT's recent performance is topping that of pre-pandemic periods and the market is rewarding that performance with a stock price that is also above pre-pandemic levels. The ultimate lesson is that a crisis will happen. How you deal with them can make your business

stronger if you continue to execute on your strategic priorities and respond to what the crisis is telling you about your approach to the business. Adversity is an opportunity to learn and to grow.

Profile Summary

Marco Sala exudes confidence, compassion, and equanimity. Most important, he and his team were ready, willing, and able to make difficult decisions attendant to the present with an eye on the future. Such a presentation conveys credibility and trust, both essential qualities in an effective crisis leader. Viewing crisis as a transformative opportunity to innovate and to be better than you ever were, as he and his IGT team have done, requires courage, an optimistic vision, decisiveness, effective communications, and trust in those responsible for implementation. This is the essence of transformative resilient leadership.

KEY POINT SUMMARY

- U.S. Army General George Patton once famously said, "The only failure in leadership is the failure to lead." Leadership is based on effective decision making. The ability to make decisions is the sine qua non of resilience-focused leadership.
- There appear to be at least four significant barriers to effective resilience-focused decision making in crisis: (a) hesitation; (b) oversimplification; (c) the failure to understand the current, latent, and long-term unintended consequences of one's decisions; and (d) impulsive actions.
- Hesitation in decision making is sometimes linked to over-analysis and the inability to link actions with consequences. A variation of the Pascal's wager paradigm can assist in moving past hesitation. Integrating dimensionality rather than all-or-none binary thinking yields more options and reduces pressure.

- In crisis, the brain is bombarded with information. To manage all these data, the brain creates information-processing short-cuts: *simplifications* or even biases. Unfortunately, these simplifications are error prone. The first step toward avoiding these errors is recognition of the oversimplifications: binary thinking, confirmative thinking, short-sightedness, and legacy thinking.

- The law of unintended consequences (LUC) states that every action leads irrefutably to unforeseen and unintended consequences. According to William Sherden (2011), "One of life's most pervasive dilemmas is the unintended consequences of our actions. Historian Daniel Boorstin observed that 'the unintended consequences of man's enterprises have and will always be more potent, more widespread, and more influential than those he intended" (p. 1). Using Pascal's heuristic in combination with improved time management will reduce adverse consequences associated with the LUC.

- Impulsive actions are based on faulty thinking processes. There are two very different styles of thinking: (a) reflexive, intuitive cognition (System 1); and (b) logical, rational cognition (System 2). System 1 thinks associatively, but it has little understanding of logic and probability and frequently makes mistakes in judgment about these. System 1 encourages us to be overconfident in what we know and fails to acknowledge the full extent of our ignorance. System 1 is activated in crisis. The resilience-focused crisis leader must counteract System 1 thinking by relying upon System thinking. Slow down, be mindful, delay irrevocable decisions, if possible, and consider the LUC.

- New Zealand's Prime Minister Jacinda Ardern demonstrated the ability to make difficult decisions in a timely and dynamic manner. Such leadership not only helped reduce the adverse impact of COVID-19 on New Zealand, but it also serves to increase the likelihood of increased foreign economic investment in New Zealand post-COVID-19.

- Marco Sala acted quickly and decisively to mitigate the adverse impact of COVID-19 on the largest gaming company in the world. But he did more. He saw the pandemic as an opportunity to bring about lasting changes that would serve to make his company larger and more profitable after the pandemic.

CHAPTER 7

EFFECTIVE COMMUNICATION

The single biggest problem with communication is the illusion that it has taken place.

—George Bernard Shaw

The first time Bryce McDonald met his platoon, they were getting back from Ramadi, and, at that time, they were the most casualty-hit unit of the war. In learning from other leaders, the first thing he acknowledged was the unit. He shared with them, "I am the CO, but you are the unit. I will learn from you. And we will set the standards high, and you will lead us to where we will go." As a leader, he listened, provided the vision, and empowered them to get there using key elements of communication.

Later, in a crisis situation, his leadership and training was transmitted to his team. While on patrol, his Humvee got it. He woke up upside down, pinned down and bleeding out. McDonald shared[1]

> I was aware that the tactics the enemy used was to hit the Humvee and then hit the secondary responder. Yet, next thing I see is that my First Sergeant opens the door. My leg is pinned in by two steel plates and halfway severed below my knee. My Sergeant looked at me and kind of chuckled. He said, 'Well, sir, we gotta get you out of here.' It was an impossible situation

---

[1] All quotations from Bryce McDonald are from an interview with the authors, June 16, 2021.

and yet he laughed and relied on his training. He and another Sergeant responded and executed with calm and even humor, relying on their training. I remembered my femur popped and the twitch being extracted. I don't know what exactly that process of resilience is . . . but love and doggedly training had a lot to do with it.

Fast-forward, this U.S. Naval Academy graduate, Marine Corps officer, and Purple Heart awardee is now the UCLA Football chief of staff. When COVID-19 hit, he again called upon his leadership and communication skills to care for his team and execute solutions to a chaotic problem set. He shared:

When I think of affecting other souls, I think of 4 Ps: Path, Place, Person, and Process. Person—helping people know who you are and where you are going; Path—guiding on a path of wisdom using space, time, and circumstances; Place—these are ever-changing and growing in life. Ideal, higher self grows into something much bigger. Discipline, accountability is key; and Process—every day I do an action; Monday—managing (e.g., walk—energy management), Tuesday—ask people questions (mental rehearsal), Wednesday (watch—revisit goals), Thursday—Micro resilience skills rehearsal (e.g., self-talk).

Yet, COVID was a disruptor. As we responded, people wanted to be anchored for next year. I tapped a rapid response planning process that got me through Covid as a leader. This was directly influenced from my training and lessons learned while serving as a Marine Corps leader. In a crisis, people need to have a plan. When things are uncertain and shifty, it's important to acknowledge that it will shift. But you must have a plan to shift from.

When COVID disrupted operations, I immediately went through an organizational anchor process. We considered first who are the main assets (e.g., medical, compliance, academics) and gathered a call with leaders from each of those departments. Our plan was that every time something new came up, we jumped on a call. We also shared messaging throughout the organization to convey optimism and this flexibility. We would literally say these phrases aloud—either "Easy Day," meaning we will figure it out or "Don't you mean a plan to shift from?" noting the dynamic, ever-changing environment.

Expert leaders such as McDonald double down on communication skills to facilitate their vision and directives. Billionaire Warren Buffet has repeatedly said one of the best investments you can make in your future is to hone your communication skills. This is especially true for the transformative resilient leader.

The University of Southern California's Annenberg School for Communication and Journalism Master's in Communication blog notes, "Communication—or a lack thereof—can make the difference between success and failure. Effective communication can inspire others to action, make a process go smoothly, and plant the seeds for new ways of thinking" (https://communicationmgmt.usc.edu/blog/4-great-communicators-and-what-theyve-taught-us/).

What kind of communicator are you? Take Self-assessment #3 in Table 7.1. Once done, transfer your scores to the summary chart in Appendix B.

FIVE ELEMENTS OF COMMUNICATION

Classic communication studies tell us there are five elements of communication: (a) the sender, (b) the receiver, (c) the message, (d) the medium, and (e) the context. In resilience-focused crisis communications, the leader is most often the sender. Those who follow are the receivers. The message must entail optimism, vision, and the decisions and directions required to allow the vision to come to fruition. The medium refers to the means or channels employed to harness the message. And the context refers to the physical or psychological

125

TABLE 7.1. Leadership Self-Assessment #3

Over the last month . . .	Seldom or never	Somewhat	Often	Almost always
11. I communicated information in a timely manner.	1	2	3	4
12. I communicated information in a transparent way.	1	2	3	4
13. I communicated information truthfully.	1	2	3	4
14. My communication was clear, unambiguous, and upbeat.	1	2	3	4
15. My communications were designed to anticipate and address the needs of others.	1	2	3	4

environment within which the message is conveyed. Let's examine each of these five elements of crisis communication.

The Sender

Let's begin with the role of the "sender" (communicating leader). Ambiguity is the mother of anxiety and distrust. Silence is the father of litigation. *There is simply no such thing as a communication vacuum. If the leader fails to communicate, someone else will—usually the most distressed.* The leader who fails to communicate in a timely manner during a crisis ignores a fundamental obligation to those who follow. In doing so, that leader abdicates their role as leader.

Information is power—share it. Communication imparts information, and information builds trust, upon which lasting leadership can ultimately be built. Many careers of promising and even well-established leaders have ended for the failure to understand one simple yet powerful maxim: *It is better to be caught in a mistake than caught in a lie.* How many influential people can you think of who made this mistake?

In a subsequent section, we address the task of crafting the message, but before that we must comment on that which precedes speaking. Contrary to intuitive thought, prior to crafting and delivering the message, it's most often advisable for the leader to *listen.* The goal of listening is to first hear, then to respond. The wisdom of hearing the distress of others actually dates to Aristotle, who wrote the first treatise on persuasion, *On Rhetoric,* in the 4th century B.C.E. This work, called the most important work on persuasion ever written, took the art, much maligned by Plato in Gorgias, to a new respectable level in Greek society. In his text, written 50 years after Plato's, Aristotle argued that before you can persuade anyone of anything using logic (*logos*), you must first hear their point of view and even hear their pain (*pathos*). In his famous 1927 prose poem, *Desiderata,* Max Ehrmann wrote "listen to others, even to the dull and ignorant; they too have their story." We believe the ability to listen to and tolerate someone else's concerns and distress is one of the highest order skills of leadership. It separates the bad from the good and the good from the great. This can be especially challenging in military or paramilitary organizations, wherein such concerns are often not well tolerated. It is a truism that the transition from military leadership roles to civilian leadership roles can be challenging largely due to the military's traditional focus upon mission, with historically little concern for the interpersonal fabric of the organization, which often rests upon listening and relationships. This is true in virtually every highly authoritarian organization, such as those in health care (Everly & Falcione, 1976), and in paramilitary organizations, such as law enforcement and fire suppression. A Cherokee proverb tells us, "Listen to the whispers and you won't have to hear the screams." This admonition seems wise even in the urgency of crisis leadership as resilience may be guided by the thoughts and voices of others.

In one of the greatest crises of the 20th century, World War II, even with time at a premium, one of the greatest communicators of his era, Winston Churchill, took time to listen rather than reflexively speak. By January 1942, the war was unfolding in such a manner that the future seemed bleak for Great Britain. Great Britain was losing the war on all fronts. In North Africa, German Field Marshal Rommel's army was advancing eastward to capture Cairo and the Suez Canal. The British colony of Hong Kong had fallen to Japanese forces, and Singapore was surrounded. There was even support in Britain's Parliament for seeking an "honorable" end to fighting. Rather than simply dictate the course of Britain's response to German and Japanese forces, Churchill arranged for 3 days of ventilation and debate. He was going to "listen."

On January 27, 1942, Winston Churchill addressed the House of Commons:

> Since my return to this country, I have come to the conclusion that I must be sustained by a Vote of Confidence from the House of Commons. . . . A Debate on the war has been asked for. I have arranged it in the fullest and freest manner for three whole days. Any Member will be free to say anything he thinks about or against the Administration or against the composition or personalities of the Government, to his heart's content. . . . We in this island for a long time were alone. . . . We are no

longer alone now. We are now at the centre . . . of 26 United Nations. . . . Whoever speaks for Britain at this moment must be known to speak, not only in the name of the people . . . but in the name of Parliament. . . . It is genuine public interest that requires that these facts should be made manifest afresh in a formal way. (Churchill, 1950, pp. 325–326)

Thus, Churchill understood that before he could ask for the endorsement of Parliament, he must first bear witness to and validate their concerns. Ultimately, Churchill was given a virtually unanimous vote of confidence. There was only one dissenting vote (464–1). So, we see a nation's response to war shaped by a willingness to listen.

In a smaller, but no less potentially grave, situation we find listening to be the foundation for hostage and crisis negotiation techniques. Psychologists from the FBI noted,

Individuals who are able to articulate clear statements of feelings are ultimately in a better position to solve their problems. Thus, in crisis intervention, actively listening to what the person in crisis is saying is vital. When a listener (negotiator) can reflect the subject's feelings, the former is perceived as being understanding. This is the basis for a relationship in which the person in crisis is ready to accept and act upon the suggestions of the negotiator, thereby resolving the crisis. (Vecchi et al., 2005, p. 538)

The lesson for the resilient leader seems clear: You must be present, and you must listen—listen to the whispers before they become screams.

In addition to the importance of listening, Aristotle argued that the credibility of the speaker is essential (*ethos*). The message for the resilient leader seems clear. Before you can persuade anyone on any matter, you must first be perceived of as a credible source.

The resilient leader brings to the communication process some form of authority or credibility. The authority can be formally ascribed to the position itself, such as rank in the military (general, colonel, first sergeant), position in the organization (chairperson, CEO, president), or elected office in a community (mayor, governor, president, prime minister). Authority can also be formally achieved by the person through merit-based promotion or informally bestowed by one's peers and earned through on-the-job performance ("street credibility"). Ideally, ascribed and achieved leadership authority are perfectly correlated. This is almost never the case, however. Ascribed authority can also be bestowed by virtue of family ties, friendships, financial investments, longevity (wherein one is promoted based on time on the job rather than based upon merit), and, of course, popularity rather than competence, as is commonly seen in politics. As noted earlier, in most cases, formally ascribed leadership would be based upon merit-based achieved leadership. If not however, of the two sources of authority—ascribed and achieved—achieved authority is the most powerful and credible in crisis. What form of authority would you have in a crisis?

The Receiver

It has been said the leadership resides in those who follow, for it is they who decide whether to be led or not. Abraham Lincoln wisely said, "Public sentiment is everything. With public sentiment, nothing can fail. Without it, nothing can succeed" (Lincoln et al., 1858/1905).

Effective crisis communications greatly influence public sentiment and the willingness to be led, but the leader's message must first be heard. Leaders are heard only when others are willing to listen. How does one decide to listen in a crisis? Integrating guidance from Aristotle's *On Rhetoric* with the extended parallel process model (Witte, 1992, 1994), we see factors emerge that significantly influence our willingness to listen:

- Leader credibility. As mentioned previously, source credibility matters. We tend to listen to credible sources of information. The message will be "dead on arrival" if the source is not credible. To be heard, leaders must be seen as credible. Always choose the most credible source to communicate the message. Share the spotlight or podium with technical experts when indicated. Share the spotlight with those who add to your own credibility.
- Leader trustworthiness. We listen to those we trust, especially in crisis, when there is little time to analyze the message. Integrity conveys trust. To be heard, leaders must be seen as trustworthy.
- In crisis, there must be a belief that there is indeed a problem. People often resist change. We often have a tough time overcoming psychological inertia, especially to do something new that might be perceived as risky. To protect ourselves against change, we might employ a psychological defense mechanism called denial, wherein we say to ourselves: the problem is not real—or not personally relevant. Denial can protect against acute psychological distress but not against real and present dangers. Many denied the risks of illness and death associated with COVID-19 in 2020–2021. Many people living in low-lying coastal areas have ignored warnings to evacuate prior to hurricanes. The outcome in both cases proved to be devastating to many. To be heard, as time permits, the crisis leader must effectively argue a viable threat exists.
- Even when there is a belief that a threat or problem exists, people must believe there is a viable solution. Otherwise, they ignore the pleas and guidance of leadership. In doing so, they

surrender their fate to luck or some other outside force. To be heard, crisis leaders must present a viable solution in a convincing manner.

- Finally, and most important, those who follow a crisis leader must believe that they personally can effectively implement the leadership guidance to address the problem. In addition, to be heard, the crisis leader must present a compelling call to action that motivates others to overcome inertia and begin.

The Message

Of the great transformative resilient leaders since the Industrial Revolution, Abraham Lincoln and Winston Churchill were two of the greatest. Not coincidentally, they were excellent orators. They had a unique skill in crafting a message. Donald Phillips (1997), in his book *Lincoln Stories for Leaders*, wrote of the 16th president, "Abraham Lincoln understood what all leaders must understand if they are to be effective; that is persuasion and inspiration, rather than coercion or dictatorship, show respect for the dignity and rights of the individual" (p. xxiv). Lincoln had a unique ability to appeal to the logical, rational aspect of his audience. Lincoln was meticulously logical. He would present both sides of an argument and lead the listener to his foredrawn conclusion. In his famous Peoria speech presenting specific arguments against slavery, Lincoln stated he was determined to be "so clear that no honest man could misunderstand me and no dishonest one could successfully misrepresent me." Reflecting on the power of words in crisis, U.S. President John F. Kennedy (1963) said, "Winston Churchill mobilized the English language and sent it into battle." Though not always popular, Churchill was known by all to speak the truth as he understood it.

As leaders in crisis intervention, each of us has been called on to guide others in their crisis response plans. During one lecture,

Everly was presenting to a group of physicians and graduate students who were interested in crisis and disaster mental health. He stated that effective messaging in a crisis or disaster was essential to resilience. A student raised her hand and asked what specific elements the message should contain. At the time, while uncertain of the specifics, he responded that fundamentally the message should anticipate the needs of people at that time and should answer anticipated questions in advance.

Later, and building on the seminal work of colleague Dr. Dan Barnett, we conducted a simple investigation to identify just how a leader should structure their message. Here are the results of our study. The resilient leader should utilize a resilience-focused crisis briefing model:

1. Describe the current state of crisis (what is happening, or what happened).
2. Describe what caused or contributed to the current crisis.
3. Describe the likely impact of the crisis, short- and long-term (physically, financially).
4. Acknowledge how followers are likely feeling and what they are likely thinking (anger, disbelief, frustration, denial).
5. Describe what actions leadership is taking (and/or will take).
6. Describe in as specific detail as possible what actions followers must take. This is sometimes presented at the strategic level (as an overview) by policy makers and at the tactical level (as step-by-step guidelines) by frontline leadership.
7. Anticipate any rebuttals and address them before the issue can be raised.
8. As might be relevant, describe what actions are being taken or will be taken to prevent such a crisis from arising in the future.

9. Emphasize the importance of collaboration and mutual support. No one is alone. No one will be left behind. Success depends upon joining together.
10. Close the message by underscoring the nature of success and/or the cost of failure.

Transformative resilient leaders can use this simple formula to craft their messaging. You can use this formula to evaluate the structural strength of any crisis messaging to which you are exposed.

The Medium

The *medium* refers to the channel, means, or methods that will be used to convey the message. It seems obvious that the leader must select the most effective means of conveying the message. In the world of advertising, for example, television is usually more effective than is traditional mail. Yet internet-based advertising is usually more effective than television. Internet-based virtual communities can be more effective yet.

Organizations such as Johns Hopkins Medical Institutions rose to the challenge in considering the multiple media of communication in response to the emergence of COVID-19. They embraced a multimedia approach as recommended before, during, and after a crisis. Specifically, it includes (a) electronic media (text messaging, email messaging) announcements and updates, (b) access to electronically stored asynchronous resources (intranet and other site-specific resources), (c) virtual and live in-person "town hall" meetings, and (d) access to virtual and live small-group discussions. Johns Hopkins' COVID-19 dashboard became a worldwide leader of COVID-related indicators, such as case rates, death rates, and immunization updates by nation, state, and local indicators.

In his book *Understanding Media: Extensions of Man*, Marshal McLuhan (1964) added a new perspective to understanding the medium that sounds like a Zen riddle. "The medium is the message," he wrote (p. 7). The nature or overarching character of the medium matters to such a degree that it, in and of itself, can send a message.

The Battle of Antietam in the American Civil War took place on September 17, 1862. Prior to the battle itself, the battle plan (Special Order No. 191) formulated by Confederate General Robert E. Lee was set to pen and paper. Amazingly, somehow a copy of the plan was left behind at a Confederate campsite and was recovered by Union scouts. This discovery served to warn the Union command of the whereabouts of the Confederate Army. If it had been acted upon by the Union command, Lee's army would certainly have met a devastating defeat. Despite initial bravado, Union General George B. McClellan was slow to act. He adopted a cautious tack, fueled in part by the thought that finding this order wrapped around three cigars was too convenient, and hence it was not a real message, but a trap. Perhaps the medium was chosen because it was meant to be discovered, the Union reasoning went. So, it was the message of potential danger inferred from the medium upon which McClellan focused and that caused him to delay, not the words written on the paper. The delay ultimately allowed Lee to avoid disaster.

More relevant to current messaging, advertisers learned that indirect observational advertising by *modeling* was far more powerful that direct advertising. The indisputable reality is that human beings learn through observation. So, if the advertiser, politician, social engineer, or transformative leader wants to change the behavior of others, they are best advised to expose them to "models," that is, examples of the desired behavior. If you want people to smoke cigars, rather than create ads urging people to smoke cigars, you will be far more successful if you simply show people going about usual and customary activities while smoking cigars. If you want people to buy a particular car, show people driving that car in a movie or TV show rather than create a more direct ad to purchase the car. In this way, many messages can be embedded in a single medium simultaneously.

The Context: The "Fog of Crisis"

The term *context* refers to the overall environment within which the communication process takes place. To promote resilience-focused leadership, understanding the context of a crisis environment is critical. As Carl von Clausewitz implied, there is the "fog of war"—so too we assert there is the "fog of crisis." The fog of crisis may consist of many of the following factors that serve to make decision making and communications difficult:

- time urgency
- ambiguity
- inaccurate, incomplete, or conflicting information
- high risk
- chaos
- increased stress physiology (fight–flight–freeze)
- the potential for System 1 thinking to affect leader decision making (see Chapter 4)
- the potential for System 1 thinking to affect the ability of subordinates to follow directives

The fog of crisis should be understood by the resilient leader as an environment wherein assumptions can be disastrous, personal values can be triggered, and the medium may become the message.

PSYCHOLOGICAL FIRST AID: A RESILIENT LEADERSHIP SKILL

We begin with this assertion: All managers should be training in *psychological first aid*. Let us explain. It probably goes without saying that physical first aid is a universally applicable skill that everyone should learn. It can be applied by a friend, family member, coworker, even a frontline leader. It can reduce acute physical distress. It can even save lives. You do not need to be a physician or a nurse to effectively provide physical first aid. Likewise, according to the prestigious magazine *Scientific American*, psychological first aid (PFA) is a skill that *everyone* should learn (Baruchin, 2015). It can reduce acute psychological distress. It can even save lives. You do not need to be a psychologist or social worker to effectively apply PFA. It can be applied by a friend, family member, coworker, even a frontline leader. The online learning platform Coursera offers a free 4- to 5-hour class on the Johns Hopkins model of PFA (https://www.coursera.org/learn/psychological-first-aid). During the COVID-19 pandemic of 2020–2021, it hosted over 300,000 learners and several million viewers.

So, what is PFA?

> Most individuals experiencing acute mental distress following exposure to extremely stressful events are best supported without medication . . . PFA is often mistakenly seen as a clinical or emergency psychiatric intervention. Rather, it is a description of a humane, supportive response to a fellow human being who is suffering and who may need support. (Inter-Agency Standing Committee [IASC], 2007, pp. 118–119)

We define PFA as a supportive and compassionate presence designed to reduce acute psychological distress and/or facilitate continued support, if necessary. PFA may be used in a wide variety of circumstances, including the stressors of daily life, at work, in family

137

problems, in cases of loss and grief, and even in disasters. PFA can be an especially useful skill at the workplace. We recall there are always two essential roles of the leader: (a) to drive and support the mission, and (b) to drive and support the psychological strength of the workforce. Every experienced leader knows that subordinates often approach their frontline managers with challenges about the work, but they will also share personal and familial issues. It is not the job of the leader to be counselor or therapist. It is the job of the leader to support the mission by supporting the psychological viability of workforce. A prescriptive paper in the *American Journal of Psychiatry* stated that "after a traumatic event, it is important that those affected be provided, in an empathic manner, practical, pragmatic psychological support" without significant reliance upon traditional mental health follow up (Bisson et al., 2007, p. 1017). The provision of PFA has been recommended by the World Health Organization, the National Institute of Mental Health, the American Psychological Association, and the American Red Cross.

While we certainly agree with the editors of *Scientific American* (Baruchin, 2015) that everyone should take a class in PFA, in this section we describe PFA and offer some insights into its application based on our work as described in *The Johns Hopkins Guide to Psychological First Aid, Second Edition* (Everly & Lating, 2022).

Step 1

Assess the impact that the immediate environment is having on the person in crisis, act to remove the person from any provocative stressors (people or things) that may be sustaining the crisis, and attend to any basic lower-order Maslovian needs (e.g., food, water, shelter, clothing, safety). Things like "taking a walk," "getting a cup of coffee," or any other diversionary process that provides the individual with some psychological distance from the source of the acute crisis or any other situation may be of assistance. Make sure it's private. Some simple things you can say to start the conversation might be "What brings you in?" or "You look like you're having a hard time, what's going on?"

Step 2

The second step involves listening. Listening, really listening, is harder than it sounds. This step in made easier by a skillful use of basic helping communication techniques. Having asked the person, "What's going on?" you now *actively listen* to their "story." The story always consists of two elements: (a) what happened (the situation) and (b) how they are reacting (thoughts, emotions) to what happened. Phrases like this might be of assistance: "OK, let's start from the beginning. What can you tell me about what happened?" A simple prompt such as "And how are you coping with this?" or, perhaps, "How are you doing now?" may be useful. The most important question you can ask at the end of this step is, "So what is the worst part of this for you?"

Be sure to listen for the "crisis triad," which is often indicative of a more severe psychological reaction. The "crisis triad" consists of

- tendencies for behavioral impulsivity;
- diminished cognitive capabilities (insight, recall, problem-solving), but most important, a diminished ability to understand the consequences of one's actions; and
- an acute loss of future orientation or a feeling of helplessness.

Step 3

Resist the temptation to rush and "fix" the problem, unless a solution is indeed readily available. It's usually a good idea to let people vent first. Once you have been told the situation and the person's reactions to the situation, especially the worst part, paraphrase what you've heard. Imagine you are a mirror of sorts. Take their words and turn them into your words to reflect the main points back. This assures them you heard the story correctly. Too often we misunderstand someone's complaints/issues, and we inadvertently make the situation worse. Use prompts like, "So let me make sure I heard this correctly . . ." or "What I've heard is . . ." When you can capture the essence of what some has been through and how they are reacting to it, especially the worst part, you begin to create a condition known as *empathy*.

According to an article by Lydialyle Gibson in the *University of Chicago Magazine* (2006),

> Empathy is one of those human impulses that defy easy explanation. It gets entangled with sympathy or compassion or commiseration; it submerges into altruism. Broadly we think of empathy as the ability . . . to imagine ourselves in the same situation [as another person], enduring those same experiences and emotions. (p. 1)

Empathy is feeling "as" someone feels, unlike sympathy, which is feeling "for" someone. Empathy fosters interpersonal connection and can empower others. Sympathy inadvertently creates a hierarchy of disconnection. Empathic communication, in this case labeling the thoughts and emotions being expressed, validates those thoughts and emotion and gives the person permission to express it. This is not to say you endorse or validate thoughts that are incorrect, counterproductive, or injurious. Similarly, this is not to say that you should tolerate an endless emotional tirade, but it does suggest that you may have to tolerate someone else's distress for a reasonable period of time.

Given the widespread endorsement of empathy in leadership training, it is not without its problems. Research (Galinsky et al., 2008) has shown problems with empathy: (a) it can be burdensome emotionally, adding to all of the other leadership burdens one might have; (b) it can sound intrusive when communicated; (c) it might blur lines of authority; and (d) a more objective understanding based on perspective taking is more effective at building a supportive connection.

Perspective taking is trying to see a situation through another person's eyes but as objectively as possible. It's role reversal without the emotional burden. It seeks to understand, not replicate, someone else's experiences. This approach to human connection was advocated by Sir William Osler, the first physician-in-chief at Johns Hopkins Hospital. Osler, considered perhaps the greatest physician of his era, recognized the emotional burden of empathy and sought to derive its benefits without its liabilities. From a leadership viewpoint, perspective taking is far less likely to blur lines of authority. The communication tool of paraphrasing is effective in fostering understanding. Understanding builds trust, and trust fosters compliance among those who follow. The children's book *Rodney Makes a Friend* (Everly et al., 2018) is a simple guide to perspective taking for children.

Step 4

Having identified the problem and their reaction to the problem, simply ask, "How can I help?" or "What do you need right now?" or "If our roles were reversed, how would you advise me?" You could say all of these things. Some familiarity with basic stress management tools can be helpful here. Perhaps the most important thing one can do in this step is to encourage a delay in any major life-changing decisions, such as leaving the job, leaving a marriage, violence, or even self-injurious actions.

Step 5

The final step in the simple PFA model is making a plan: "So, where do we go from here?" If you believe other resources are required (e.g., human resources department, employee assistance program, peer support program), help the person make a detailed plan on how to access those services.

PROFILES IN TRANSFORMATIVE RESILIENT LEADERSHIP: Franklin D. Roosevelt, President of the United States

During his four terms as president of the United States, Franklin D. Roosevelt (FDR) faced many challenges. The first was to inspire citizens and Congress to do what was necessary to overcome the Great Depression.

Background

While most remember FDR as the U.S. president during most of World War II, his role as a visionary transformative leader began soon after his diagnosis with a crippling disease. In 1921, at the age of 39, FDR was diagnosed with poliomyelitis (polio). The disease paralyzed both of his legs, leaving him unable to walk. In 1924, he sought treatment from the warm mineral springs at a rehabilitation facility in Warm Springs, Georgia, then owned by George Peabody. So impressed was he with his improvement and the potential to aid others, he bought the facility and the 1,200 surrounding acres in 1926. His transformative vision was to create an international destination that would be the only rehabilitation facility in the world to specialize in polio. His vision was realized. His role as optimistic visionary leader continued immediately after his first election as president of the United States in 1932 (he was elected president four separate times).

The Crisis/Challenge

At the time of his election, the country was suffering from the Great Depression, with over 12 million Americans out of work. This constituted roughly one third of the available workforce. Intensifying the fiscal trauma, capital investment dropped by roughly 90% in 1932. In short, the United States faced a paralyzing financial crisis in 1933 by the time of FDR's inauguration. His predecessor, Herbert Hoover, had refused to act to avert the imminent collapse. It was a time that demanded resilient crisis leadership.

Actions Taken/Lessons Learned

Roosevelt understood he needed to communicate directly with the American people to instill hope and share his vision. Knowing the hardships Americans had endured and would endure, Roosevelt harnessed the power of the "bully pulpit" (a term coined by FDR's cousin, President Theodore Roosevelt) and delivered an inaugural speech that would serve as a foundation for building a virtual culture of resilience:

> This great Nation will endure as it has endured, will revive and will prosper. So, first of all, let me assert my firm belief that the only thing we have to fear is fear itself—nameless, unreasoning, unjustified terror which paralyzes needed efforts to convert retreat into advance. The people of the United States . . . have registered a mandate that they want direct, vigorous action. They have asked for discipline and direction under leadership. They have made me the present instrument of their wishes. In the spirit of the gift I take it. (Roosevelt, 1933)

FDR had a bold plan for the economic recovery of the United States, but like Lincoln he knew that no such plan could prevail with positive public sentiment. Simply said, this plan hinged on the trust and support of the American people. On March 12, 1933, he instituted a series of radio speeches famously known as "fireside chats." These chats were a means of continuing to mitigate the erosion of trust in government by communicating his optimism and further building a culture of resilience. He gave 30 such fireside radio chats lasting from 11 to 44 minutes each from 1933 to 1944. His chats informed his constituency of the what, why, and how of his optimistic vision for a full economic recovery.

FDR realized he had two constituencies: the public who elected him and the Congress and state legislative assemblies with which he would have to work. So, FDR worked hard to communicate his optimistic vision to federal and state lawmakers. On Sunday, March 5, 1933, FDR met with Congressional leaders to enlist their support for a bold, if not radical, action. FDR proposed closing the American banking system, understanding it was broken beyond repair in its current state. The next day he met with governors from throughout the United States to explain his decision. He reportedly received a standing ovation from the bipartisan group.

On Monday, March 6, at 1 a.m., President Roosevelt issued an executive order declaring a bank "holiday." Consistent with his upbeat approach, he rejected Herbert Hoover's term "moratorium." The order caused the immediate suspension of all banking transactions. This order effectively shut down the banking system throughout the country and basically "rebooted" the entire system, this time with safeguards that would prevent a similar crisis from ever happening again.

As noted in Chapter 2, the bank holiday as envisioned and instituted by FDR was just the first of a series of dramatic changes to American life called the New Deal. The term "New Deal" was borrowed by FDR from a 1932 book written by one of his economic advisors, Stuart Chase. The New Deal consisted of an evolving series of transformational programs designed to reform and revitalize America. Perhaps most important, it was designed to provide hope for the future in the wake of a society and a democracy that had nearly collapsed.

Ironically, FDR reportedly admitted that his vision for recovery, reform, and revitalization was fueled by a personal optimism but lacked detail. Thus, it was always a work in progress. At times, his relentless optimistic drive to realize his ultimate vision was more important as a motivating force than was any realized milestone success. That said, of greatest importance to the theme of this chapter on communications is without a supportive "public sentiment"; without the enthusiastic support of the electorate, Congress, and state governments, the New Deal would likely have failed. The requisite support was engendered and assured because of FDR's skill as a transformative resilient communicator.

Profile Summary

So far, we see that transformative resilient leadership consists of having a positive optimistic vision at what may be the worst possible time and acting in a decisive manner amid uncertainty and the fog of crisis. But more is needed. Leadership consists of not only having an optimistic vision but also communicating the vision and the subsequent decisions in a compelling manner so that those who follow can understand the vision, gain strength from the vision, and ultimately act on it. FDR was a virtual prototype of such a leader (Goodwin, 2018). Simply said, no one leader in modern history exerted more influence on the trajectory of the United States than did FDR.

KEY POINT SUMMARY

- The University of Southern California's Annenberg School for Communication and Journalism states, "Communication—or a lack thereof—can make the difference between success and failure. Effective communication can inspire others to action, make a process go smoothly, and plant the seeds for new ways of thinking." Billionaire Warren Buffet has repeatedly said one of the best investments you can make in your future is to hone your communication skills. We believe this is especially true for the resilience-focused crisis leader.
- The process of communication conveys the leader's optimistic vision and the directions for helping the vision come to life.

- "There is simply no such thing as a communication vacuum. If the leader fails to communicate, someone else will . . . usually the most distressed." The leader who fails to communicate in a timely manner during a crisis ignores a fundamental obligation to those who follow. In doing so, that leader abdicates their role as leader.
- Classic communication studies tell us there are five elements of communication: the sender, the receiver, the message, the medium, and the context.
- Contrary to intuitive thought, prior to crafting and delivering the message, it's most often advisable for the leader to listen. A Cherokee proverb tells us, "Listen to the whispers and you won't have to hear the screams."
- Abraham Lincoln wisely said, "Public sentiment is everything. With public sentiment, nothing can fail. Without it, nothing can succeed."
- Effective crisis communications greatly influence public sentiment and the willingness to be led, but first the leader's message must be heard. Leaders are only heard when others are willing to listen. The extended parallel process model informs us how to maximize the impact of our message: (a) describe the problem, (b) describe the prescribed solution, and (c) persuade your constituency they can affect the solution.
- Crisis leaders should adopt a crisis briefing approach that, among other things, (a) describes the current state of crisis (what is happening), (b) describes what caused or contributed to the current crisis, (c) acknowledges how followers are likely feeling and what they are likely thinking (anger, disbelief, frustration, denial), (d) describes what actions leadership is taking (and/or will take), and (e) describes in as specific detail as possible what actions followers must take.

- In conveying a message before, during, and after a crisis, it is usually best to employ a multimedia approach.

- Given that people learn more from observation than rhetoric, transformative resilient leaders must directly and indirectly demonstrate the change they want others to adopt. Be the change you want to see in the world.

- A fundamental leadership skill is psychological first aid (PFA). PFA may be defined as a parallel to physical first aid with the goal of stabilizing acute distress, mitigating acute distress, and facilitating access to continued care as indicated. According to *Scientific American*, PFA is a skill that *everyone* should learn. It can reduce acute psychological distress (Baruchin, 2015). It can even save lives. You do not need to be a psychologist or social worker to effectively apply PFA. It can be applied by a friend, family member, coworker, even a frontline leader. The online learning platform Coursera offers a free 4- to 5-hour class on the Johns Hopkins model of PFA.

- FDR is profiled in this chapter as a transformative resilient leader. We assert the key to his success was that he understood that without a supportive "public sentiment," without the enthusiastic support of the electorate, Congress, and state governments, his game-changing New Deal would be likely to fail. The necessary support was engendered and assured because of FDR's skill as a transformative resilient communicator.

CHAPTER 8

SUPPORTIVE RELATIONSHIPS

Supportive relationships are a force multiplier.

—Unknown

On May 19, 1967, during his 75th mission (and 5 days before he was to come home), Captain J. Charles Plumb's plane was shot down in North Vietnam. He survived the crash and was captured and held as a POW in a communist Vietnamese prison for over 5 years and 9 months. Later, as shared in an excerpt from his chapter "Packing Parachutes," his impact as a transformative resilient leader did not stop there:

> I sat down in a restaurant in Kansas City not too long ago. About two tables over a guy kept looking at me and I didn't recognize this gent and he stood up.
>
> This guy walked over to my table and looked at me and said, "You're Captain Plumb."
>
> I looked up and I said, "Yes, sir, I'm Captain Plumb."
>
> "You're that guy. You flew jet fighters in Vietnam," He said. "Part of the Top Gun outfit out of Miramar, California, you were shot down off the aircraft carrier Kittyhawk, you parachuted into enemy hands. You spent six years as a prisoner of war."
>
> Somewhat dumbfounded, I looked up at this guy and I said, "How in the world did you know all that?"
>
> He finally broke into a smile and said, "Because, I packed your parachute." (Plumb, 2017)

Plumb's story has been highlighted in leadership books and programs across the world. He continues to challenge us to consider how our chute packing is going. Who is looking to us for strength in times of need? And who is lifting you up when you feel the odds are against you?

Leadership is the glue that keeps a team, an organization, or a society from dissolving into a chaotic crowd, especially in crisis. The wise leader harnesses the power of group cohesion and supportive relationships both inside and outside of the organization. Our own research cited earlier in this book discovered relationship formation as a key predictor of effective leadership. Supportive relationships benefit the crisis leader in at least two ways.

First, in the worst of times, the leader needs to mobilize the added strength of others for support and even collaboration to accomplish the mission. Over 2,000 years ago in his *Metaphysics*, Aristotle asserted that "many things have a plurality of parts and are not merely a complete aggregate but instead some kind of a whole beyond its parts." This notion has come to be known as synergy. *Synergy* may be defined as the interaction or cooperation of agents to produce a combined effect greater than the sum of their separate parts or effects. In a sense, the powerful impact of synergy may propel the team through crisis and toward growth with a strong offensive.

Second, during the worst of times the leader needs someone to "cover their back," as well. Consider this to be the defensive strength of supportive relationships. A transformative resilient leader's strong relationships with their team facilitates the team's ability to efficiently attend to the most critical elements of the crisis. The team is not just empowered but relies on the trusting, reciprocal relationship to defend and strengthen the primary leader's direction.

So, consider: Who's got your back? How supportive are your relationships? Table 8.1 provides a brief self-assessment. When complete, transfer your score to Appendix B in the back of this book.

TABLE 8.1. Leadership Self-Assessment #4				
Over the last month . . .	**Seldom or never**	**Somewhat**	**Often**	**Almost always**
16. I was confident my friends and family would be supportive, if necessary.	1	2	3	4
17. I made a conscious effort to reinforce the supportive relationships I have.	1	2	3	4
18. I was confident my team would "have my back," if necessary.	1	2	3	4
19. I made a conscious effort to reach out to establish supportive connections.	1	2	3	4
20. I did not hesitate asking for help if and when needed.	1	2	3	4

Note. From the Resiliency Science Institutes, LLC, 2020. Reprinted with permission.

THE POWER OF INTERPERSONAL RELATIONSHIPS

John Donne, writing in 1624 noted, "No man is an island, entire of itself . . ." In their groundbreaking book, *Stress, Health, and the Social Environment*, sociobiologists James Henry and Patricia Stephens (1977) asserted that one of the core sociobiological drives in the human brain is the drive for social affiliation and attachment, that is, the need to belong. The drive to belong to a group (to be part of something greater than oneself) is a core human attribute. The need for affiliation was described by the eminent psychologist Dr. David McClelland as a core human motivation to be associated with and belong to groups of allied others. This affiliative/attachment drive may manifest itself in various forms of interpersonal collaboration and reliance, coalition formation, mentoring, collective achievement, and even play (collective recreation). The study of interpersonal affiliation and social relations became McClelland's life work. He chaired the Department of Social Relations at Harvard University from 1962 to 1967. McClelland was first Everly's advisor, then mentor, and later friend. At least once a month, they would have lunch and discuss topics of mutual interest. Somehow, in every conversation, he would raise the importance of human cooperation and collaboration. He traveled the world promoting these processes. He agreed with the sociobiologists of the time that the affiliative drive was "the cement of society."

But affiliation is more than a form of social cement. History teaches that safety, strength, and superior creativity are derived from collaborative groups. The most feared warriors of the classical Greek era were the Spartan *hoplites* (citizen soldiers of the city-state of Sparta). The hoplite was trained from the earliest age to be a warrior. His primary weapons were the sword (*xiphos*), the spear (*dory*), and the shield (*hoplon*), all used while fighting in a formation called a *phalanx*. Of these weapons, the shield held the greatest meaning. Why? The phalanx was a formation wherein Spartan hoplites stood shoulder to shoulder in a tight formation with shields overlapping. This overlapping of shields meant two things. First, that individually one's shield protected not just oneself but also the hoplite to one's left. Second, the aggregation of overlapping shields created one solid offensive and defensive wall, a virtual war machine and embodiment of Aristotelean synergy.

Let us move from ancient Greece to Roseta, Pennsylvania. McClelland argued that the drive for affiliation fuels human health. The pioneering research of Dr. Stewart Wolf would prove that assertion to be true. Wolf was one of the founding fathers of the field of psychosomatic medicine, which is the field of medicine that studies the influence of psychological processes on physical health. When asked which one of his research projects or discoveries was the most meaningful, he said it was the discovery of just how powerful the influence of social factors actually is on human health, rivaling, in his opinion, the power of the human genome.

Wolf conducted an amazing 25-year investigation on the health of the inhabitants of Roseta, Pennsylvania. Roseta was a medical marvel. Its inhabitants possessed significant risk factors for heart disease, such as smoking, high cholesterol diets, and a sedentary lifestyle. Despite these risk factors occurring at a prevalence equal to surrounding towns, the inhabitants appeared to possess an immunity to heart disease compared with their neighbors. The death rate from heart disease was less than half that of surrounding towns! Dr. Wolf discovered that the protective factor was not in the water nor the air but was in the people themselves. Research revealed that social cohesiveness, a family-oriented social structure (in which three generations routinely resided in the same household), and emotional support imparted immunity from heart disease. With the advent of the suburbs and the dissolution of the three-generational households, mortality rates in Roseta increased to rival surrounding communities.

Last, connection to others can foster calm and personal well-being that can serve the crisis leader. In his 1889 essay *Aequanimitas*, Sir William Osler, the first physician-in-chief at the Johns Hopkins Hospital wrote, "From staying connected with others, there grows a sense of equanimity." Equanimity is certainly an essential aspect of crisis leadership. If the crisis leader is to foster resilience—not merely bouncing back but transformationally bouncing forward—the support of others is essential. Indeed, research has shown interpersonal support to be the single best predictor of human resilience (Flannery, 1990; Ozer et al., 2003). So, we see that fostering collaboration and support not only adds cohesion but may also propel a group to greater successes than ever before.

COVID-19 AND THE NAVAJO NATION

It is the job of the transformative resilient leader to build an organizational culture of resilience wherein support and collaboration are inherent in the culture itself. The Navajo Nation exemplified this fact in their response to the COVID-19 pandemic. Consisting of over 300,000 people, the Navajo Nation is the largest of the 574 Native American nations residing within the borders of the United States. By September 1, 2021, although only about 52% of nonnative Americans were fully vaccinated against the COVID-19 virus, well over 80% of members of the Navajo nation were vaccinated, potentially approximating herd immunity. At the core of the Navajo advantage resides the same factor that is the core of transformative resilient leadership— a focus beyond the immediate crisis, a focus on the future.

The COVID-19 pandemic disproportionately affected economically disadvantaged populations, rural populations, and minorities. Native Americans were disproportionately adversely affected. Public health authorities around the world learned there was value in testing, contact tracing, and, of course, in vaccine administration. Two significant challenges faced Native American public health officials: the logistics of testing, tracing, and vaccine administration; and an initial skepticism. The skepticism stemmed from a long history of distrusting nonnative Americans, going back to the arrival of European settlers, who brought smallpox to the Americas and in doing so killed over 90% of the Indigenous population.

So, how did the Navajo become so successful at vaccine administration given the logistical challenges and potential skepticism? The key resides in a value system that recognizes the power of collective interdependence and prioritizes the well-being of the collective. According to Leonela Nelson, a researcher at the Center for American Indian Health and member of the Navajo Nation:

> It's embedded in our values that we don't just think about ourselves. . . . We think about others and the generations that are going to come after us, so getting the vaccine is just one small thing that we're able to do to ensure that life goes on. (Powder, 2021, para. 6)

In an interview with Jackie Powder for the Johns Hopkins Bloomberg School of Public Health, Allison Barlow, director of the Center for American Indian Health, addressed the logistical challenge:

> They used a lot of creative methods to get vaccines out to their communities that included everything from vaccine blitzes to door-to-door campaigns. Indian Health Service teams embedded with folks from our Center's community health representatives, would literally go door to door with mobile units . . . and provide shots.

As far as overcoming psychological challenges, Barlow continued:

> I think there were three key influencing channels. There was a lot of focus on the elders and what our ancestors did to get us here, and it's now our responsibility to carry on, and the way we do that is to protect all of the community. There were also a lot of youth-led campaigns, with the youth saying we need to protect our elders. In tribal communities, both elders and youth are viewed as sacred. The youth are the future, and elders are the keepers of the past and keepers of the codes, the culture, and traditions. The third was having Native American doctors and nurses speak out with their expert knowledge.

In a 2021 press release, Navajo Nation Vice President Myron Lizer said,

> Together, we are overcoming the COVID-19 pandemic one day at a time. The strength and resilience of our people has been demonstrated each and every day. As we emerge from the pandemic, we must continue to take precautions even after being vaccinated and keep supporting one another. Most importantly, please continue to pray for our people, our health care workers, and those who have lost loved ones. (The Navajo Nation, 2021, para. 4)

FIVE LEADER CHARACTERISTICS THAT FOSTER CONFIDENCE AND INTERPERSONAL SUPPORT

So, how can you tell if your organization or group possesses an organizational culture of resilience? This section describes five characteristics that define the organizational culture of resilience as we have observed over the last 4 decades.

Equanimity

"Thou must be like a promontory of the sea, against which, though the waves beat continually, yet it both itself stands, and about it are those swelling waves stilled and quieted." Sir William Osler quoted this passage in his famous 1889 address entitled *Aequanimitas* (imperturbability). He went on to say:

> In the first place ... no quality takes rank with imperturbability ... Imperturbability means coolness and presence of mind under all circumstances, calmness amid storm, clearness of judgment in moments of grave peril. ... It is the quality which is most appreciated by [those who look to you for guidance].

Osler noted that the leader who becomes "flustered and flurried in ordinary emergencies, loses rapidly the confidence" of their constituency.

He also noted that this sense of imperturbability is often misunderstood. It can be misconstrued as a cold and aloof attitude, when it should be the assumption of an objective perspective without a "hardening of the heart."

Reliability/Trustworthiness

Think of reliability as consistency. Consistency yields predictability. Predictability engenders trust. Trust is a key characteristic of high-performing organizations, especially those enduring a crisis. Collaboration, even synergy, is based upon trust. According to Paul Zak (2017), people who work in "high trust" organizations have 74% less stress, 106% more energy, 50% higher productivity, 13% fewer sick days, 76% more interpersonal connectedness, and 29% more life satisfaction, compared with those who work in low-trust organizations. The resilience-focused leader must remember: Promises do not have expiration dates. Do what you say you will do. If a promise must be broken, always explain why. Show genuine kindness to others. People will judge you by the way you treat others. People will eventually hear whatever you say about them—say kind things, be complimentary whenever you can. *One of the most important ways to manifest integrity is to be loyal to those who are not present. In doing so, we build the trust of those who are present* (Covey, 2004).

Accepting Responsibility for Your Actions

Accepting responsibility for your actions as a leader projects integrity and further builds trust. And yet it is rare. So rare is it that accepting responsibility for your actions, especially your mistakes, approaches countercultural status. Over the past 2 decades, we have sadly seen the emergence of a well-intentioned but highly destructive trend of coddling and overprotection of our youth, according to the authors of the brilliant award-winning book *The Coddling of the American*

Mind (Lukianoff & Haidt, 2018). This trend has given rise to a virtual generation or more of individuals who have difficulty taking responsibility for their actions. In their search to displace responsibility, they inadvertently surrender control of their lives by blaming others, blaming bad luck, or blaming other external forces. The greater one's ability to displace responsibility, the weaker one's sense of self-efficacy and collective efficacy become. This is anathema to the crisis leader.

Honoring Others

One of the jobs of the resilience-focused leader is to build a community of supportive and collaborative individuals. Help people feel part of something greater than themselves. One of the greatest gifts you can give another person is to honor them, recognize their work, and help them feel important. Though it's hard to believe, no matter how accomplished the person, acknowledgment is always appreciated. And as William James noted, "The deepest craving of human nature is the desire to be appreciated." That said, share the credit for the successes of the collective. Shared success is a powerful mechanism to create a shared identity and a supportive and collaborative collective. Publicly acknowledge success. Emphasize the importance of teamwork.

Mentoring

Mentoring is a tradition with a 3,000-year history. It is a process wherein the mentor (leader) provides consultation and guidance to the follower (mentee). Homer wrote of this process in the *Odyssey*. Odysseus entrusted his son to be cared for by a trusted friend and advisor: Mentor. Mentoring can exert powerful effects. Dr. E. E. Werner (2000, 2005) conducted a 40-year longitudinal study of

698 infants on the Hawaiian island of Kauai—all children born there in the year 1955. One third (210) were at high risk from developmental adversity, yet one third of those did well decades later. Two key factors that emerged as protection from adversity were (a) a strong bond with a nonparent caretaker (mentor) and (b) support from a peer group. The resilience-focused leader should provide those who follow with the opportunity to develop their own expertise. *Expertise* may be defined as knowledge plus experience. Create buddy and mentoring systems in which the less knowledgeable or experienced can learn from the more experienced. Create teams wherein the less knowledgeable or experienced can learn from those with greater expertise. The mentor must advise, counsel, and sometimes provide corrective criticism. The mentor should employ constructive criticism, however. Criticism should never be viewed as punitive. Criticism should always be accompanied by suggestions for remediation. The resilience-focused leader should strive to create a collaborative environment in which criticism and even failure are accepted as opportunities for growth. Your ability to constructively change a life is that which will make you immortal.

Here is a final admonition. Crisis can challenge group cohesion. Sensing the urgency and pressure of crisis, it is not uncommon to see a leader shift leadership styles from participative to autocratic. In some instances, such a shift is essential to survival. In others, however, doing so can cause the leader to lose the strength of identification and personal investment of the collective team. This weakens the team, weakens the leader, and reduces the likelihood of success.

RECOGNIZING AND AVOIDING "TOXIC" PEOPLE

In building supportive relationships, not everyone in the collective team or organization wants to contribute or even participate. The leader will prosper from heeding the advice of Max Erhrmann, who in 1927 wrote in his poem *Desiderata,* "Exercise caution in your business affairs; for the world is full of trickery. . . . But let this not blind you to what virtue there is; many persons strive for high ideals; and everywhere life is full of heroism." The challenge resides in distinguishing trickery from virtue.

During Everly's professional training, he was fortunate to study with one of the world's leading experts in human personality, Dr. Theodore Millon at the University of Miami and later Harvard Medical School. He taught that until one understands a person's personality, it is hard to truly understand who they really are. So, what is personality? *Personality* can be simply defined as one's relatively consistent patterns of thoughts, emotions, and actions. The search to understand the personality of the serial killer was the task undertaken by the FBI's famous Behavioral Sciences Unit in Quantico, Virginia. In studying personality, it is striking how there exist so many genuinely kind, supportive, and compassionate people. On the other hand, we would be remiss if we didn't also mention those who possess "toxic" personality patterns—certainly not as toxic as those of the serial killer but toxic in other ways.

People displaying such patterns have an ability to spread unhappiness and dysfunction. They ultimately have a propensity to poison personal relationships, professional relationships, even entire careers. Here are descriptions of seven potentially "toxic" personality patterns that can create crises, erode resilience, and undermine organizational goals. By *toxic,* we simply mean the kind of people who, through their behavior or attitudes, present obstacles to a healthy, resilient working environment. Manifesting toxicity may range from passive noncompliance to actively undermining the leader and the mission. Their actions can be even more toxic during a crisis, as they cannot be fully relied upon to support resilience initiatives or may actually fuel the crisis.

The "Negative/Complaining" Person

Did you ever work with someone who seemed chronically pessimistic and negative? They have a unique ability to see the negative in almost anything. They never seem really happy and appear to complain incessantly. Nothing is ever good enough for them (that's the negative part), and they are more than willing to let you know about it (that's the complaining part). When you first meet them, they appear pleasant on a superficial level, but the longer you know them, the more their behavior becomes interspersed with an often obstinate or manipulative quality. When asked to do something they don't really want to do, they respond with "Yes, but . . ." They resist innovation and change of almost any kind. Consistent with the notion "misery loves company," they have mastered the use of passive–aggressive behavior as a means of making everyone else as unhappy. In general, they are cynical and pessimistic and can even be obstructionists. These people can actually be dangerous, in the sense that they tend to be very self-defeating, doing things that get themselves and others into trouble as they express their displeasure with life. Believe it or not, these folks are very controlling. This personality style never really learned how to take charge of their own life in a constructive way, so they take charge in self-defeating, passive–aggressive, manipulative ways. But the major reason they are so dangerous is that they self-destruct their careers and interpersonal relationships. The leader and the organization could be collateral damage.

The Narcissist

The narcissist is self-centered ("It's all about me"). They are interested in others only to the degree that they can benefit from a relationship. They have no desire nor intention to pursue a reciprocal relationship. When the usefulness of a relationship has ceased, the narcissist will seek another relationship. This applies to employment as well. The recurrent question they ask is, "What's in it for me?" As arrogant and self-centered as these individuals appear, their behavior usually masks a deep sense of insecurity for which they spend a lifetime trying to compensate. It is not uncommon to see these individuals "collect" things, even people, that they can show off as examples of their success. So-called trophy spouses, exotic cars, large homes, yachts, and expensive jewelry can all be part of this person's "collection" designed to convince themselves that they are "worthy." Don't get us wrong; there is no problem in acquiring nice things. The problem is when the process of acquisition is really the never-ending quest to compensate for felt insecurity. Narcissists "use" people and things and then discard them in this never-ending cycle of compensation. They do not recognize interpersonal boundaries, as everything is considered theirs for the taking. They are prone to severe midlife crises.

The Social Butterfly

The social butterfly craves attention. To satisfy this craving, they cultivate relationships. The more the better. On the surface, they appear to be a real "people person." They can be flirtatious, overly dramatic, and risk taking. Often the life of the party, they can be charming and exciting. They often judge themselves and others by external criteria, that is, what they have, how they look, who they know, and can be incessant "name droppers." They can get frustrated, angry, and even depressed if they do not feel they are getting the attention they require. Sadly, almost all of their relationships are superficial. They move from one relationship to another as easily as the butterfly glides from one flower to another, never staying longer than necessary to extract nourishment. The social butterfly's appetite for attention is insatiable, however. As such, they can be flighty and unreliable. They can leave in their wake broken promises, disappointed acquaintances and coworkers, and even broken hearts.

The Aggressive–Selfish Person

They seem to act consistent with the mantra, "What's mine is mine; what's yours is mine." Thus, an aggressive–selfish person is exactly that: aggressive, selfish, and controlling. These individuals tend to be adventurous and risk taking. They are superficially charming and glib. They are exciting. Inclined to be possessive, verbally abusive, and even physically abusive, they tend to be controlling and intimidating towards other people. They seek out "friends" and partners who will "need" them. They tend to see themselves as assertive, rather than aggressive. They have a sense of entitlement, which leads to a remarkable selfishness. As a result, their entitled selfishness extends to usurping the rights of others as if it was their God-given prerogative. They are known to use intimidation as a mechanism for controlling other people. Rules, and even laws, are acceptable only if they do not keep them from doing something they want to do, otherwise such rules and laws are seen as not being applicable to them. They tend to get angrier as they get older. If they have children, they often develop conflicts with their children, as their children age and their control over their children lessens. The children ultimately recognize these parents as controlling and distance themselves. These parents then see their children as ungrateful.

The Control Freak

Psychologists use the term *anankastic* to describe a compulsive person who is preoccupied with rules, orderliness, and control.

They have a penchant for detail and are often meticulous. They strictly adhere to rules and regulations and can be very controlling. Rules are rules, no exceptions. They tend to be highly rigid. They abhor change and are prone to anxiety. They avoid emotional interactions. They have a disdain for the unpredictable. They can be prone to paralyzing obsessive thoughts and even behavioral rituals. Careers that require an attention to detail are ideal for this person, while careers that require creativity, emotional expression, empathic communications, and flexibility will usually be extremely stressful. The anankastic person does not perform well in crisis absent a predetermined set of crisis-response protocols. In rare situations, this person can be quite emotionally brittle, wherein crisis can lead to extreme controlling actions and even violence.

The Frenemy

A frenemy is someone who, on the surface appears to be your friend, but actually hopes you will experience unhappiness and failure in relation to themselves. Frenemies are insecure and unhappy people; thus, they hate your success, as it reminds them of their own failures. They make themselves feel better by helping those who are worse off. It's not an altruistic motive, it is a way of compensating for their own chronic dysphoria by feeling superior to another, at least temporarily. Ironically, when you are experiencing significant distress, they will often be the first at your side providing genuine support. It is only when you resolve your challenges that their true angry and jealous nature emerges. Even then they are not outwardly aggressive, they are passive–aggressive (aggressive in subtle, stealth ways).

Here are seven ways to recognize a frenemy (see *The Cut* online magazine article at https://www.thecut.com/article/how-to-spot-frenemies.html for a detailed discussion of frenemies):

1. They criticize others behind their backs, and they do the same to you.
2. Their jokes are hurtful, but when challenged they say they were only kidding and that you are being too sensitive.
3. They take advantage of your friendship whenever possible.
4. Although insecure and racked by feelings of inferiority, they project a presence of superiority.
5. They only want to talk about their achievements and friends, while name-dropping incessantly.
6. They resent and therefore publicly diminish your achievements.
7. They disguise cruel criticism as constructive feedback, but when challenged they say they were just trying to be helpful.

Type A Behavior Pattern

The last person on our "avoid if possible" list is the Type A. Type "A" sounds good, doesn't it? Wrong! In the mid-1970s, two Stanford cardiologists, Ray Rosenman and Myer Friedman, wrote a book titled *Type A Behavior and Your Heart.* In that book, they discussed years of research that documented that a certain consistent behavior pattern could dramatically increase the risk of coronary heart disease. The link between this behavior pattern and arteriosclerosis was so strong it was recognized by the National Heart Lung and Blood Institute of the National Institutes of Health as a risk factor for premature heart disease. So powerful was this toxic pattern on one's health, it was considered as pathogenic as smoking cigarettes.

165

They called that pattern Type A, and it is characterized as being generally hostile, combative, workaholic, and prone to coronary heart disease. That said, in a book on leadership, we are less interested in arteriosclerosis than in the effects of Type A behavior on the psychological climate of the workplace. It would appear that such behavior exerts a destabilizing effect on esprit de corps and overall group cohesion.

The Type A pattern consisted of a classic "workaholic" syndrome:

- Unrelenting time urgency. Chronically in a rush, even if there is no objective reason to be in a rush. They are in a chronic state of time urgency, rushing around only to wait. They hate crowds, lines, and people who take their time when speaking. They will even finish sentences for people who speak too slowly.
- Multitasking, always doing more than one thing at a time. This is technically called polyphasic behavior.
- Competitive—very competitive. They seem compelled to make a win–lose situation out of everything. And they are very poor losers, so much so that they are often hostile toward others if they lose.
- Impulsive. Type A individuals hate to wait and are eager to act. They will often act without thinking or planning. Seldom do Type A individuals take time to read directions—they just act.
- Chronic hostility. Research sought to identify which of the aforementioned factors was the most "toxic." Evidence suggests that underlying all four is chronic hostility. The hostility appears to emerge from a deep sense of insecurity, and the "win at all costs" attitude of the Type A may be an attempt to compensate for that insecurity.

To be clear, these characteristics are not binary—all or none. Rather, they are dimensional and often situation dependent. The full-blown enduring Type A pattern in the aggregate is relatively rare. Even so, such behavior in the workplace can undermine leadership and resilience.

SUMMARY

This list of toxic people is by no means exhaustive but instead serves in the aggregate as a warning to the resilient leader that not everyone on the team is willing or necessarily able to be a team player. A psychologically toxic environment can be devastating to morale, the mission, and resilience. It can exacerbate crises and even create them. It has been our experience that setting clear policy and procedural expectations for performance must include not only specific mission-related task functions but working within and contributing to a psychologically healthy climate. This is difficult, however, as it may be hard to demonstrate and or quantify. The organizations we have studied that have been most successful in creating an organizational culture of resilience have relied less upon policies and procedures and more upon an unspoken expectation of mutual respect, collaboration, and mutual support that seems to permeate the environment and that is informally reinforced by the attitudes and actions of the peer culture as well as the resilient leader. All leaders would likely benefit from training in how to recognize "toxic" people in order to inform effective selection, development, and in some cases, separation decisions.

In this chapter, we have tried to make the case that collaboration and support are essential to the success of most organizations. The art of not only harnessing but enhancing the interpersonal resource of any organization or community is not easy. The ability to transformationally lead through crisis using the power of the community to create enhanced growth and prosperity is a rare attribute, as we've mentioned throughout this book. Here is an excellent example of transformational resilient leadership that embraces the importance and power of community.

PROFILE IN TRANSFORMATIVE RESILIENT LEADERSHIP:
Jim McCann, Founder, 1-800-FLOWERS

Jim McCann[1] is an entrepreneur, but more than that, he is also an industry icon who, like Jon Luther (see Chapter 5), transformed his industry. Jim became a florist when he bought and managed a chain of flower shops in New York. He grew that business into a multimillion-dollar enterprise.

Background

When Jim purchased the name 1-800-FLOWERS, everything changed. Under the banner of 1-800-FLOWERS, he pioneered selling flowers and related gifts by telephone and the internet. In 2014, moving beyond his success in the floral industry, his company bought the famous but struggling food gift retailer Harry & David. Up until recently, Jim was a minority owner of the New York Mets professional baseball team. Jim once described his success to me (Everly) as "catching lightning in a bottle." While such a description connotes a rare occurrence, it belies Jim's astute understanding of the importance of cultivated relationships and the power of community. As a leader focused on resilience and transformation, Jim not only cultivates the social fabric of his businesses and charities, he continues to find innovative ways to harness the human side of enterprise. In the time I've spent with Jim, I've found him to be not only an innovator focused on transformation but a gentleman who exudes unwavering compassion.

The Crisis/Challenge

Previously, we looked at the impact of the pandemic on two very diverse sectors: public health and the international gaming industry. Given the

---

[1]All quotations from Jim McCann are from an interview with the authors, May 27, 2021.

pervasive and devastating impact of the pandemic, we now examine the COVID-19 recession in retail sales:

> Spending all of 2020 in a relative state of chaos . . . retailers have been more focused on stopping the bleeding than looking ahead. Few companies have had the ability to make investments for the future in the past twelve months, and that will impact the space going forward. (Salpini, 2021)

Austerity programs have been implemented by many retail sales organizations. While most retailers struggle to simply stay in business, the pandemic may also serve as an opportunity for those focused on resilience and transformation.

For 1-800-FLOWERS, the pandemic provided an unusual combination of difficulties and opportunities. As Jim described it:

> Our company's mission has always been to help people express themselves and connect to the important people in their lives. During the pandemic, we found that we were uniquely positioned to expand upon that mission. In the poignant greetings accompanying many gifts we shipped, we saw how people yearned to be together. We saw an opportunity to support those connections. Yet, this required the seamless continuation of our business operations under the stress of the pandemic, magnified by increased demand for our services. We also needed to imagine new ways of connecting with our customers and to offer opportunities for them to remain close to their loved ones, in spirit if not in person. During COVID, we've continued to deal with all the day-to-day challenges of running any business, plus pandemic-related price escalation, labor shortages, increased freight costs, and lower productivity, to name just a few. However, COVID wasn't the only serious unforeseen challenge. In early fall 2020, the beautiful Rogue Valley of southwest Oregon, home to our Harry & David brand, was hit with the devastating Almeda wildfire, destroying acres and acres of land across Oregon and more than 1,000 homes.

Actions Taken/Lessons Learned

Both 1-800-FLOWERS and Harry & David market goods that have a unique ability to fuel human connection. Jim explained:

> Like other businesses, we'd developed plans for the emergencies we knew we might face one day. But no one expected a pandemic. Like everyone else in our industry, it just wasn't in our playbook. All crises have lessons to teach. COVID-19 was no exception. So, what did we learn?
>
> First, we had to organize an enterprise-wide response plan. When COVID-19 struck, we assembled our Pandemic Preparedness and Response Team, led by our general counsel, Michael Manley. This team provided guidance on continuity of operations through the analyses of health-related information and economic trends as they emerged in real time.
>
> Second, the pandemic underscored the importance of communications. With facilities or personnel in approximately 40 states and some 5,000 team members, clear communication is critical to our company, and that's been especially true during the pandemic. As many of our team members started working from home, we had to enhance our communication technologies so they could do their jobs.
>
> Third, unlike other recessions, physical health and safety became a key challenge. For those who must report to an office or warehouse, implementing public health guidelines in a timely fashion has been critical. In a time of such uncertainty, we've worked to maintain good company morale and we recognized that was often related to health concerns. The rapid, accurate dissemination of information was and is crucial.
>
> Fourth, supporting our partners has always been key to our success, but even more so now. We partner with the best florists in each community we serve, and the pandemic was very hard on many of these small businesses, which are so important to our service to our customers. We introduced support

programs with a package of broad financial relief measures, provided PPE, and assisted in the transition to contactless delivery. When the health emergency began, we made it a priority to support safety net organizations nationwide by providing nearly $1 million in product donations from our foods brands. More broadly, as food insecurity rose, we enlisted our customers at Mother's Day and during the year-end holiday season for philanthropic campaigns, donating $100,000 to No Kid Hungry to provide up to 1 million meals for children. Also, our Local Heroes campaign worked with local florists to create bouquets honoring frontline workers.

In this book, we have emphasized the importance of building an organizational culture of resilience. Jim described what that looks like:

As a result of the Rogue Valley fires more than 100 of our employees lost their homes and possessions. We served meals to them and their families in our cafeteria and worked to find new housing. Our employees across the country donated nearly $150,000, which the company matched. The leadership of Steve Lightman, Group President, Gourmet Foods and Gift Baskets, exemplified the type of leadership that augmented the resilience of all our team members. We learned how important support and connection with our own team could be. One story, in particular, struck me. In fall 2020, the day after the Oregon wildfires broke out, our chief of staff/ VP, Meredith Weinberg, told me of a previously scheduled virtual meeting that had been on her calendar with some Harry & David colleagues. Meredith had reached out to cancel it, recognizing the tremendous challenges that team was under, professionally and personally. The response she got was "the meeting will go on"; the team was committed to staying on track with taking care of our company and our customers. One team member participated from her car since she did not have access to her office or home.

In Chapter 1, we described the power of adversity to be transformative, to create opportunities and even growth. Jim's experiences underscore that assertion. McCann describes in detail his company's transformative response to the pandemic:

Fifth, and perhaps most importantly, we learned to understand the crisis of the pandemic as a change accelerant here at 1-800-FLOWERS.COM, Inc. The pandemic accelerated the pace of change in planning for our future. It made what might have happened over the course of 5 years happen in just one. Public health rules forced us to close the 40 Harry & David retail stores across the country, not knowing how long they would be closed or if and when people would come back to stores. We then made the painful decision to close them permanently and sought to find opportunities for those team members impacted.

It has been a transformational time for our company. We have now seen significantly increased consumer demand and new customer growth. We have gained added appreciation of our loyalty program, Celebrations Passport, and have grown it appreciably. We are making the transition to a new e-commerce technology platform. Under the vision and leadership of Tom Hartnett, Group president, consumer floral and gifts, in August 2020, we welcomed into our family of brands PersonalizationMall.com, adding a leading provider of personalized gifts and home décor to our platform. Under the leadership of my brother, Chris McCann, our president and CEO, various groups of team members remained focused on the business operations during the pandemic; other teams continued in their roles of looking ahead to how we had—and still—wanted to evolve as a company.

Prior to COVID-19, we were working to transform our relationship with our customers in ways that would create a real sense of community between us and our customers. Meredith and I had been chatting, prior to the pandemic, about our vision for earning customer loyalty. There are lots of marketing terms and metrics around customer acquisition but we were looking for something different, something about the genuine connection and relationships we want to earn with our customers. I recall Meredith saying, "We are not after customer acquisition; we want to build relationships. Jim, we want relationship acquisition!" I loved that distinction and that term. And we set out to earn and deepen those relationships in new and genuine ways. We got to work on strategies and specific initiatives and hired Robert Tas as our first chief growth officer to assist with this transformation. Under the leadership of Melissa Owen, director of growth marketing in our floral brand, we expanded our resources on sympathy. We desired to be a genuine resource to our family of customers in what may be their greatest moment of need. The change in how we looked at sympathy also helped us look at our other products and services differently. So as a direct result of the pandemic, we initiated seven new programs to bring us closer to and help us better support our family of customers:

1. Connectivity Council. When COVID-19 hit, Larry Zarin, our board member, encouraged us to gather experts on helping our customers to express themselves and connect with others. We put together the Connectivity Council, to help our community by exposing them to wonderful minds around wellness, mental health, and relationships. Why would a gifting company develop a Connectivity Council? We've learned how connection is the single best predictor of human resilience. So, we wanted to foster it using input from recognized thought leaders.

2. Celebrations Pulse. We launched this weekly note from me and CEO Chris McCann to our customer community, providing tips and resources for navigating the health crisis together, speaking with customers in more engaging ways, simply checking in on them to see how they were doing. These emails rarely discuss our products. We are proud that over 7 million members of our community receive them.

3. Connection Communities powered by Wisdo. We introduced this peer-to-peer community that helps guide people through meaningful life events by connecting them with others who have walked the same path—like coronavirus anxiety, self-care, coping with loss, motherhood, relationship advice, and caregiving. We provide complimentary access to Connection Communities to our customers and have a quarter million participants. We thought a lot about how we could expand the use of online meeting places to foster the sense of community that so many of us were missing.

4. Collaborating with workshop provider Alice's Table, we launched live, virtual floral and cheese and dessert charcuterie interactive classes just six weeks into the pandemic. Thanks to the hard work of Loreen Entenmann on our team, as well as everyone involved in the project, so far, more than 50,000 people have joined in, and we are excited to bring other offerings to our customers.

5. Breakfast at Wolferman's Bakery. This new morning show centers on our Wolferman's brand. It offers a mix of our guests' most delicious recipes, helpful tips, and opportunity for people to just "chat" over a 30-minute breakfast because who has an hour for breakfast?

6. Summer 2021 introduces Celebrations Book Club by Cheryl's Cookies, a new, virtual program combining fun summer reads, connections with authors, and our wonderful Cheryl's Cookies brand.

7. Finally, a Harry & David Hosted Dinners program, which brought guests to a table of curated menus using our products, successfully went virtual.

As for the future, our transformation into a stronger engagement company, more in tune with our customers and poised to provide them with growing connection opportunities, has been the silver lining for us in a time of great challenge. We learned that the vision we had prior to the pandemic was the right vision for our company and our customers. We became more of what we wanted to be, because of the pandemic and despite the pandemic. The COVID-19 pandemic was and is a tragedy, but we take some solace in the fact that we were able to become the company that truly helps our customers during moments big and small, celebratory, and sad.

Profile Summary

Jim McCann is a transformative crisis leader who understood the power of connection and how it could be harnessed not only to mitigate the impact of adversity but to "bounce forward"—accelerating positive change and revealing opportunities unknown prior to the COVID-19 pandemic. As he shared, "As devastating as COVID-19 was, for businesses focused on fostering connections between people, it also was a crucible. The pandemic was transformative, the proving ground for new approaches to building and sustaining community." The actions taken are obviously relevant to one aspect of the retail sales industry but serve as examples of transformative thinking and application. Jim's visionary business acumen is obvious, but we believe it is his genuine caring, compassionate, and supportive presence that will resonate with his employees and customers in such a manner as to outshine the myriad business successes he has had and will have in the future.

KEY POINT SUMMARY

- Research has shown that the single best predictor of human resilience is the support of others.
- Research has also shown that one of the best predictors of leadership effectiveness is relationship building.
- The organizational culture of resilience is based on relationships. It is a culture that is characterized by mutual respect, collaboration, and mutual support, especially in crisis.
- Supportive relationships serve the crisis leader by mobilizing the power of synergy (the whole is greater than the sum of its parts) and operating as a threat surveillance system.

- You can recognize a resilient culture because its members have shared goals and aspirations for the collective. There is the belief in the necessity of reciprocal support and collaboration. There is a belief in collaborative interdependency wherein the success of the individual is intertwined with the overall success of the organization. The members of the organization possess shared values in terms of how the organization's goals should be achieved. There exists a high degree of cohesion. And group members identify with and show pride in their affiliation with the organization's brand.
- The resilient leader fosters the growth of supportive relationships by demonstrating equanimity, reliability, responsibility, appreciation of others, and mentoring.
- Not everyone on the team is willing or necessarily able to contribute to a healthy, resilient workplace. Some may exert a "toxic" effect on the collective. Thus, the leader must be wary of "toxic personalities." Such personalities can erode the psychological well-being of the group and in doing so compromise the mission.
- It has been said a true friend reaches for your hand and touches your heart. The transformative resilient leader should surround themselves with those who exude integrity, compassion, and unrelenting support.
- Jim McCann, founder of 1-800-FLOWERS, is a transformative resilient leader who understands more than most the power of human connection. His companies are deeply invested in establishing connection and community.
- The Navajo Nation had extraordinary success in getting its citizens vaccinated in response to COVID-19. A cultural value system that sees its elderly and its youth as precious resources that must be protected may be the key to success.

CHAPTER 9

INTEGRITY

It takes 20 years to build a reputation and five minutes to ruin it.
—Warren Buffet

Consider the collective power of leaders such as former Secretary of State Henry Kissinger, former Defense Secretary William Perry, former Senators Sam Nunn and William Frist, former Chief Executive Officer of Wells Fargo & Co. Richard Kovacevich, and former Director of the Centers for Disease Control William Foege. Add to the list former a U.S. Navy Admiral and former U.S. Marine Corps General who went on to serve as a Defense Secretary in the Trump Administration. This collection of influence and resources could help transform the world. Indeed, when all of these individuals joined forces to support a startup biotech company run by a bright young Stanford University dropout, they hoped that this company would live up to its promise of transforming health care. That company was Theranos, and the founder and CEO was Elizabeth Holmes.

Holmes famously raised over $700 million in venture capital for her company by networking and building relationships, and she managed to get all of the aforementioned influential and resourceful leaders into a powerhouse board of directors. Holmes claimed that her company, Theranos, had developed a revolutionary blood-testing device that could perform hundreds of tests, even complex genetic analyses, with only a single drop of blood from a finger prick.

Yet, without a foundation of a leader's integrity, the power of a collective is eroded and can wreak devastation. The foundational cracks were exposed in 2015, when Pulitzer Prize–winning journalist John Carreyrou broke the story in *The Wall Street Journal*: Theranos was built on a culture of lies and intimidation (Carreyrou, 2015). Not only did the device not work but patients were being harmed when they made medical decisions based on the device's inaccurate test results. In the January 2022 federal fraud trial, Holmes was found guilty on four charges of defrauding investors. At the time of this book's publication, Homes faces up to 20 years in prison for each of the counts and a $1 million dollar fine.

Integrity may be defined as the consistent practice of truthfulness and honesty, a fidelity to a moral compass. Integrity is the cornerstone of trust, and trust, as noted in the previous chapter, is essential to building supportive and collaborative relationships. Honorable leaders earn the trust, respect, and affection of their followers, inspiring them the desire to "return with honor," satisfaction, and inner peace, rather than regrets. Across time, the significance of integrity has been highlighted. In his treatise *The Prince*, Machiavelli (1534/2006) proclaimed that the leader who shows integrity is not easily conspired against. He further noted that no matter how much benefit a leader subsequently bestows upon those who follow, the pain and angst of betrayal linger a lifetime. It can spell his demise. Last, let us recall the famous words of the fictional crisis leader Maximus, "What you do today will echo for eternity" (from the movie *Gladiator* [Scott, 2000]).

It seems clear that how a leader treats those who follow is an imperative to success. When the leader treats those who follow with kindness, compassion, and integrity, the mission takes care of itself. The challenge for the transformative resilient leader is leading through crisis with an eye on future development. Winning in the moment, while important, is not everything. Sacrificing the future for

TABLE 9.1. Leadership Self-Assessment #5				
Over the last month . . .	Seldom or never	Somewhat	Often	Almost always
21. People viewed me as honest.	1	2	3	4
22. People knew I could be trusted.	1	2	3	4
23. I was consistent and reliable.	1	2	3	4
24. People viewed me as fair.	1	2	3	4
25. I acted with integrity.	1	2	3	4

Note. From Resiliency Science Institutes, LLC, 2020. Reprinted with permission.

the present is unacceptable to the leader. Leading with honesty and integrity is an investment in both the present and the future. Take a moment and complete self-assessment #5 in Table 9.1. The higher your score the better—but be sure to be honest in your responses! Then transfer your score to Appendix B in the back of the book.

In this chapter, we examine the nature and importance of integrity to the transformational resilient leader.

FOUR DEADLY SINS

"In looking for people to hire, you look for three qualities: integrity, intelligence, and energy. And if they don't have the first, the other two will kill you," noted Warren Buffett, CEO, Berkshire Hathaway. We believe that there are four "deadly sins" that undermine integrity and leadership effectiveness. While one may weather a slight transgression or misstep in navigating crises, we see the gravest of consequences when leaders engage in one of these behavioral patterns. Regardless of whether it was the initial decision or the ones that followed, leaders who acted more in accordance with these "sins" rather than a "moral compass" ultimately experienced catastrophic outcomes.

Lack of Candor

Having those who follow respond urgently and faithfully to success-fully navigate adversity begins far before the actual order is issued. Effective compliance resides within an atmosphere of trust. Trust is dependent upon understanding and integrity. The leader who has successfully built a culture of integrity by truthful, transparent, and timely communications (i.e., candid communications) will reap the benefits; the leader who has not will suffer the consequences.

Communicating lies is of course the most egregious action a leader can take to destroy any sense of candor. But communicating half-truths and withholding information are other (and far more common) means of leading with a lack of candor. Creating a climate and culture of candor is certainly more of a challenge than simply reading these recommendations and nodding your head. Too often and even with good intentions leaders withhold information with seemingly "compelling" justification. Yet, effective crisis leaders take deliberate action to create and sustain transparency.

Specifically, they *embrace truth telling*. In crises, leaders who share accurate information contribute directly to building a cushion of resilience in the climate. Team members are not only smart but often highly informed in ways leaders can only imagine. Especially in crisis, people can quickly discern half-truths, and while they may not have the accurate picture as they fill in the blanks with their own creative ideas, the crisis becomes compounded with a climate of distrust and fear. Instead, effective crisis leaders who tell the truth, cultivate a climate where followers are more willing (not less) to make sacrifices for the organization, give extra effort, and extend themselves personally to help the team and leader achieve their mission.

Crisis leaders also create *organizational structures that support candor*. Team standards that promote truth telling are frequently verbalized, including rewarding contrarians and protecting whistleblowers, diversifying sources of information, offering internal idea-sharing opportunities, and having open-door policies. Shifting systems towards candor, if the history is otherwise, is a daunting task, and executives are rarely selected for this ability. Yet, especially in times of crisis, this skill set is a requisite to accomplish the mission and take care of the people.

Selective Acceptance

The second deadly sin relates to one's acceptance of success. Successful leadership relies on the foundation of the team. At its simplest understanding, one would not be a leader if not for the team—there would be no one to lead. Indeed, it takes all members of the team to accomplish the mission and overcome hurdles presented in a crisis. *Selective acceptance* refers to when a leader either (a) accepts credit for the successes of the team without acknowledging the efforts of others or (b) is quick to accept the credit for success and/or is conspicuously absent when there are failures.

Navy Seals have a specified Seal Ethos (Naval Special Warfare Command, n.d.) that clearly describes the values and standards of being part of this elite special forces unit. A section directly subscribes, "I do not advertise the nature of my work; nor seek recognition for my actions." In his University of Texas 2014 Commencement speech, Admiral William H. McRaven, ninth commander of U.S. Special Forces

Command, shared inspiring life lessons learned from Navy SEALS Basic Training (BUDS). One of the lessons centered on the value of surrounding yourself with people to help you succeed. He shared, "You can't change the world alone—you will need some help—and to truly get from your starting point to your destination takes friends, colleagues, the goodwill of strangers and a strong coxswain to guide them."

Accepting the credit for the successes of your team without acknowledging the efforts of others will slowly destroy your village around you. Over time, people will grow disillusioned, at best, in pushing forward to overcome a hurdle and then receiving little to no acknowledgment for their sacrifices. Admiral McRaven highlights an indisputable fact: You will not overcome a crisis on your own, so best acknowledge all who made it possible.

In NCAA and professional sport, elite sport psychologists are often reluctant to take interviews or be highlighted in providing the mental coaching for the team or individual performers. Yet, there also exists another group of mental skills consultants who look to leverage the connection to a team and market this connection to gain credibility, and of course, another contract. Coaches, in both the mental and sport domains, have long recognized that their offering is only one part of what contributes to the performance of an individual coach or team. The successful sport psychologists agree— if you are going to take credit for the individual or team success, you must also "own" the failures. Selective acceptance ("cherry-picking") by leaders taking credit for only the successes and then dismissing or avoiding ownership of any missteps or failures decimates integrity and the resilience of climate and team.

Failure to Take Responsibility

As mentioned in the previous chapter, taking responsibility earns trust. And, as described in considering the pains of selective acceptance, failure to take responsibility destroys trust. Blaming others as a means of avoiding responsibility further compounds the pain of crises. Rather, successful leaders take a balanced critique of processes and outcomes from decisions. They evaluate these actions nonjudgmentally to evolve the team positively. This is perceived to be an opportunity to learn and use the reflection as rich data that leads to considerations of not only what was effective and will continue to be so, but also what was ineffective and needs to change. By embracing all events as opportunities to learn, even failures, successful leaders strengthen the resilience of the team and increase successful outcomes.

This deliberate commitment to learning and taking responsibility is best exemplified by an after-action review performed by many military units. One of the finest, the U.S. Navy Blue Angels have documented their after-action debrief process, where each team meticulously reviews the operation—down to each second of the command calls. Each team member, including the squad leader, reviews their individual performance and highlights each call, response, and action that may not have been perfectly executed. This high standard of critical review and learning from each aerial maneuver is critical to evolve the technical and tactical performance of this elite team. Poor execution, even if lasting only 1 second, could result in catastrophic outcomes. At the conclusion of an individual pilot's debrief report, the pilot responds with "Glad to be here." This signifies to the team that they acknowledge the mistake and are committed to taking deliberate action to ensure that it is corrected and does not happen again. Regardless of rank and position, the collective trust and resilience of the Blue Angels team is strengthened by this candid, direct, and radical acknowledgment of responsibility.

Beware the leader who accepts responsibility in name only. How many times have you heard something like the following? Recently, we heard a leader quote Harry Truman and say in the wake of a failed operation, "The buck stops here." The next words out of his mouth were to blame others.

Beware the leader who accepts responsibility for problems but then does nothing to solve them.

Beware the leader who says, "OK, so maybe there was a failure. What difference does it make?"

Cheating

Breaking rules to gain unfair advantage, or cheating, is a clear-cut way to undermine successful leadership. And unfortunately, the stories of lying and cheating are rampant across industries—sport, business, government. What is consistent across the stories illustrates that often the transgressions of leaders were not one-off incidents but rather extended over periods of time. From the USA Gymnastics failings of leadership to protect girls and women from a sexual predator (and resulting in a $250 million settlement against them) to the notorious fraudster who ran the largest Ponzi scheme in history (worth about $65 billion), lying and cheating behavior becomes an insidious disease that will destroy people and organizations. Successful business leaders will note that *there are no shortcuts to making money*. Any shortcuts that involve lying and cheating will undermine the sustainability of the organization and compromise the leader's abilities to navigate crises effectively.

ACTING WITH INTEGRITY: IT'S A PROCESS

To mitigate these deadly sins, successful leaders facilitate the development of organizational standards. For example, in the military, success, most simply, is defined as the completion of the mission and taking care of its people. Yet, to be an effective crisis leader, one needs more than a values card sort or online legal training. Successful transformative resilient leaders engage in a continued process that is guided by moral development.

Dr. Joe Thomas (USNA Class of '61), chair and distinguished professor of leadership at the U.S. Naval Academy and past director of the John A. Lejeune Leadership Institute, Marine Corps University, is an international leadership expert who shares on the topics of leadership and ethics regularly throughout the United States, Europe, Africa, and the Middle East. He has identified four stages of moral development in military leaders: Compliance, Moral Understanding, Moral Maturity, and Moral Ambition (Thomas, 2014). As he shared, these stages are not new but iterations from those cited back to the Roman Centurion. Compliance is more narrowly reduced to behavior modification than to understanding the role of a leader. There are those who follow out of fear of consequences or those who resist critically thinking and challenging through the problem set. Many never shift to the next level—Moral Understanding—as it requires one to be assertive rather than passive. Thomas (2014) noted that "the most important transitory step from the role of follower to that of leader is to step from compliance to moral understanding" (p. 4). Given the influence of our values in our decision making, it is critical for leaders to clarify their values, align their actions to this compass, and communicate this to their team. This is an ending quest, as moral understanding is regularly revisited to facilitate deep understanding with the team. This evolves to Moral Maturity, where the leader embraces continuous evaluation of their beliefs and understanding how those beliefs manifest in actions. Thomas identified Moral Ambition as the ultimate stage of moral development. He noted that this reflects the active pursuit of virtuous behavior not only for oneself but one's affiliations as well. This requires tremendous courage, reflection, and dedication. While few leaders achieve this stage, those who do are noted as ones who were able to change the world.

Lastly, high-performing leaders recognize that facing tests of integrity are guaranteed. Engaging in self-development to identify one's values, align the organization's values to standards, and take action that is congruent with this compass is challenging, tireless work. Effective leaders embrace this process as an opportunity for growth rather than a threat to self, position, or power. They anticipate potential conflicts and seek consultation to find accountability when challenges arise. As Dr. Ken Ravizza, a pioneer sport psychologist, has said, successful leaders "get comfortable with being uncomfortable." This process is not for the weary but for one who is committed to living as a successful crisis leader.

The Foundation of Values

Before outlining team or organizational values, effective leaders reflect and identify their personal values. Indeed, values are the foundation of character and behavioral choice. Values influence actions both in times of regular operation and crisis. Social psychologists Verplanken and Holland (2002) highlighted that those values only influence action if they are activated. They argued that self-reflection raises one's awareness of one's values, which are therefore more likely to be activated when decisions or actions take place.

Leadership experts offer various exercises or processes to facilitate values clarification. Each may offer varying opportunities to reflect and build one's self-awareness. Values clarification is more than a feel-good moment or identifying that which sounds best in the company email signature block. It is an ongoing process rather than a check-the-box engagement. Effective crisis leaders have peeled back through self-reflection, even if uncomfortable, and can clearly state the foundational values that shape them. And they routinely revisit these same questions to explore whether their values have shifted given life developments.

To identify values, one method is to do a computer search to find a comprehensive list of values. Select 10 to 15 words that most resonate with you. Then rereview those words, noticing which might be subcategories of others, and refine your selection down to five values. In reviewing the five selected, ask yourself, "Which three can I not live without?" These top-three values can be prioritized and illustrate the core of who you are and what you stand for.

Another method starts a values exploration by considering the following fundamental questions:

- What is most important to you?
- If you could select three words to describe yourself, what would they be?
- What values must you have in your life to feel fulfilled?
- What challenges you or stretches you the most?

Now, ask yourself, "Why?" Write down your answer, then reflect on your response and again ask yourself, "Why?" Dig deep here. This is not a check-the-box exercise but a deeper exploration of why something truly is a foundational element of who you are and what you stand for. If you want to go deeper, keep challenging yourself by asking, "Why?"

Understanding what is critically important to you will shape the directions of response and how you will lead your team when a crisis hits the fan. Beyond critical decisions, values also shape decisions made for key determinations of organizational standards, goals, and priorities.

A Moral Compass

Transformative resilient leadership directs action. We would be remiss if we did not drive this conversation to action. Indeed, reflecting to build awareness is a critical foundation block and analyzing experiences can aid in this discovery. Yet, there are numerous examples of failed leadership where an organization's leaders lacked integrity in their actions. Many scandals reveal that individuals recognized concerning behaviors and were uncomfortable with the path forward yet did not step forward or speak up in action. Organization members are perceptive and will be swayed by the slightest perception of deceptive action—and the outward outcome can be catastrophic. The initial crisis may then become insignificant compared to the catastrophe of a cover-up.

Gentile (2010) suggested taking a leadership development approach called Giving Voice to Values (GVV) to emphasize *action*. In an effort to consolidate habits of response informed by one's values, GVV challenges people to consider when and why they act in alignment with their values and to identify factors that enable or undermine them from doing so. The acknowledgment of biases or avoidance tendencies is deliberate to not only raise awareness but also to recognize these behaviors as potential levers in problem solving when ethical conflicts arise. Considerations of conflictual situations are critical, and to develop effective action plans, people are encouraged to pause and reflect. Keep in mind the protagonist's response to the situation rather than jumping straight into identifying "What would you do?" that could be influenced by rationalization or resulting cognitive dissonance that could dissuade them from taking appropriate action. After identifying the protagonist's response, people are then encouraged to consider creative solutions for implementation. Deliberately charting a course of action that is anchored in one's values can lead to decisions being more effective and transformative.

Yet leaders may be facing a critical situation without the opportunity to fully explore the path as outlined above. At the most basic level of consideration, crisis leaders acting with integrity must consider the following questions:

- Am I being deceptive?
- Does my action hurt anyone?
- Would I be comfortable if those I loved (e.g., partner, children) learned of my actions?
- Would I be hurt or angry if someone did this to me?

Due to the dynamic conditions crisis leaders often face, situations requiring ethical decision making are ever-present. Indeed, these are not one-off conditions where the leader can "make the call" and then go home. Odds are, there is another decision to make immediately following. In this process, the ability to review and analyze the impact of the previous decision is often critical. The opportunity to learn from the process creates invaluable data points for the leader to integrate to face the next challenge. To review, ask yourself, "What went well?" or "What could have been done differently to improve the outcome (both intangible and tangible)?" The dynamic condition of the crisis will require constant shifting on the part of the leader. Yet, the foundation of values and acting with integrity will make the navigation smoother and more efficient.

PROFILES IN TRANSFORMATIONAL RESILIENT LEADERSHIP: Mike Candrea, Legendary NCAA Coach, Olympic Champion

Legendary head coach Mike Candrea, one of the greatest coaches in the history of college athletics, announced his retirement following the 2021 season. After 36 seasons at the University of Arizona, Coach Candrea has left a legacy that will live among the greatest coaches in college history. His achievements underscore a record of success almost unparalleled by any program in any sport at any level.

Background

At the time of his retirement, Candrea was the NCAA all-time leader in wins for the sport of softball. The iconic coach enjoyed more than three and a half decades of unparalleled success at leading the Arizona softball program. Candrea finished his career with a 1,674-436-2 (.793) at Arizona. Candrea teams won eight national championships, and he has been named National Coach of the Year four times. Under his leadership, 53 of his players attained All-American status, earning 108 such designations in total. In 2019, Candrea won his 1,600th career game, achieving that distinction more quickly than any coach in NCAA history in any sport, at any level. Only three coaches in any sport have more NCAA Division I victories than Coach Candrea. In addition to his dominance at the collegiate level, Candrea also spent time internationally with USA Softball. He served as the head coach of Team USA's medal-winning softball teams in the 2004 and 2008 Olympics. The team earned gold in Athens in 2004 and silver in Beijing in 2008. Under his leadership in 2004, the team posted a perfect 9-0 record, outscoring its opponents 51-1 on its way to a gold medal in the most dominant team performance in modern Olympic history. Coach Candrea has also served as a consultant to Major League Baseball.

The Crisis/Challenge

The sports contested on the playing fields are meant to teach not only excellence in athletic performance but also life lessons regarding winning, losing, and (most relevant) resilience. It is a truism that athletics serves as a training ground—even a metaphor—for life. At first glance, the challenge faced by Mike Candrea for over 36 years will seem quite different from those challenges faced by others profiled in this book, but we suggest that at its core, it's much the same. The coach's pursuit of excellence in athletic performance, with the greater goal of preparing student athletes for futures beyond athletics, is like but more challenging than the challenge facing a corporate leader preparing junior associates for careers in the same field. The lessons learned through intensive coaching and mentoring on the athletic field teach powerful lessons about life itself. Perhaps as best captured by the words of iconic sports broadcaster Jim McKay, "the thrill of victory . . . and the agony of defeat . . . the human drama of athletic competition" can shape the future for all involved. Candrea was not one to back down from a challenge. Daily, he challenged his players, and when it came to drawing up the schedule of opponents, his philosophy was no different. He built his schedules to be the most challenging in the country. The challenges he faced over his groundbreaking career were many—from coping with personal loss 10 days to performing on the world stage to being the shoulder many could lean on when facing their personal adversity and still being called upon to perform.

Actions Taken/Lessons Learned

How does a leader best prepare those who follow to perform at the highest levels while at the same time preparing them for the inevitable challenges that will follow, now and in the future? According to Coach Candrea,[1]

> You have to take care of the person more than the athlete. That is my guiding light. . . . I have always been a people person. That helps when you are in tune with people first, and then task outcome second. It's all about getting the right people in the culture. When a crisis hits, you have to go back to your grassroots of family—why you are important to me and me to you. How much you care about people and how you treat people. Being able to put the task at hand aside knowing if you don't take care of this person, you will never be able to achieve the outcome. I have always worked backwards; you find out you can never get to the task at hand until you treat the person.

---

[1]All quotations from Mike Candrea are from an interview with the authors, June 14, 2021.

When asked how exactly one cares for the person more than the athlete, Candrea responded,

> I have always tried to be very open, very honest, and compassionate. Vulnerable and sharing my experiences with them. And I think the more you do that, and when something really big happens, then it is easier to have the tough conversations. Usually they (the players) are intimidated when they walk into my office. And, then they realize the conversation is going to be a different one. We end up talking about what is going on for them.
>
> I had to redefine my success in this job because at one time, I thought my success depended on winning and championships. I realized I couldn't have any longevity if I only had that outcome. The most important thing for me is that I prepare them for life—outside of softball. They have to have the ability to navigate through failure and tough times so they could make decisions on their own and they would be safe and wouldn't have to depend on anyone in life and they knew what it took to navigate the trials and tribulations we all go through.

Candrea's approach in coaching has paid off in expected ways. His success in competition is legendary, but it is his success off the field that now resonates most with him:

> I was a new college graduate coaching and teaching for the first time. Early in my career, my wife and I lost a child, three weeks old. I had no insurance and all I was thinking about was the money. The baby was in intensive care, and I was thinking, "How am I going to pay for all of this?" And so, I go back to my upbringing and my faith and how I treated people. People reached out to me because of how I treated them. They helped me get through it. They supported us through it.
>
> Later, when I lost my wife, Sue, 10 days before the Olympic Games in 2004, I didn't know if I could still be a coach.

I didn't know if I could fit the bill in the biggest moment of my team's life in the Olympic games. These kids wanted me to be there for them. But because of how I treated them, they ended up being my safety net to get through all of this. It was the first time I realized how important how I treat people really was, not just because of the outpouring of support from the players and family, but it came from the entire world. It was the first time I realized I was making an impact because they became the help I needed to get through a difficult time. Softball was my savior. I never dreamed of softball playing that role. I had a chance to move forward or backwards and sit around feeling sorry and saying why me and 10,000 questions. Truthfully, the outpouring of the people whose lives I impacted positively carried me. I was a father-away-from-home, a mentor, someone who they found really cared and listened.

Candrea learned several lessons from his experience coaching:

Focus on your people. My whole mission in life as a leader is to prepare young people for when crises happen to them in their life. We go through life thinking nothing bad will happen, and when it all of a sudden happens, and it will happen, preparation is the key. So, you better start preparing them to be able to handle that. When people say I care, it means I was there for them, to help them navigate it. On the field, coaching is about 10% of what you do, 90% of what you do is time you spend is on promoting the well-being of those you coach.

I think consistency in life is important. Consistency is important in being a role model. I always wanted to be that model who may not have all the answers, but I'll try to find them if I can. I wanted them to live through my actions. When you do that, I realized that the biggest fear I had was disappointing them. It flipped everything. Some don't want to disappoint me, but they didn't realize how much I didn't want to disappoint them. I never would want to disappoint them.

Tolerance and acceptance are important. When I think about leading, I think you should be able to lead everyone. Not just the people who tell you what you want to hear, also, the ones that tell you what you don't want to hear, literally and otherwise. I had to do it in my own life. My son Michael is into tattoos. It had an effect on me and how I expressed my feelings. Almost put a guard up. People are unique and different, and if you don't take time to get to know people and understand that you will miss the boat on golden nuggets of people and who they really are.

Tolerance for the gray areas in life is important. Understand if you are going to lead, it's hard to lead if everything is black and white, all or none. A lot of what we do is gray.

Availability is crucial. Good leaders are available. Do you truly have an open door? Or just on your terms. Sometimes you don't want to deal but there's no good time when someone needs your help. Can you help them feel that you care and you are genuine? I have had struggles with that because I was always at work. If a player called, I would drop everything.

Consistency is the foundation of honesty. I have always wanted to be as consistent as I could be for the women I was leading because they were on a roller-coaster (navigating the challenges of college and competing). The last thing I wanted them to deal with is not knowing where I was.

Most important is treating people with honesty and integrity. At the end of the day, I wanted to do it right. It's not the numbers. The numbers kinda happened. Nothing is guaranteed, you won't make perfect decisions. As long as you make them where your heart is in the right place, that's what I have tried to do. Because at the end of the day, your guiding light is making life better—not the game, not this moment—but life in general.

Profile Summary

Coach Candrea's career is perhaps best summarized by the words of Pericles (ca. 450 B.C.E.): "What you leave behind is not what is engraved in stone monuments, but what is woven into the lives of others" (Parker, 2006, p. 118). Such an approach to athletic leadership clearly paid dividends. A case in point was the 1991 season. Arizona finished 11–9 and fourth in their conference. Disappointing to say the least and tied for Candrea's worst regular season finish. Given his schedule, the team was selected for postregional season competition. Entering postseason play as an underdog, Arizona finished by winning the regional championship. The next step was the College World Series. When the series was over, Mike Candrea and his team earned their first national championship.

At the time of his retirement in 2021, Coach Candrea was the all-time-winningest coach in NCAA softball history and ranked fourth of any coach in any NCAA sport with 1,674 wins. His University of Arizona softball program won the National Championship eight times, and he coached USA Softball to a gold and silver medal in 2004 and 2008, respectively.

Yet throughout his retirement celebrations, including the naming of the Mike Candrea Field at the University of Arizona's Hillenbrand Stadium, former players, coaches, staff, and loved ones all honored a greater achievement—the man who transformed lives. As Arizona's All-American and Olympian Pitcher Jennie Finch shared, "We're just so thankful for who he is and what he's done, and he's done it the *right* way. . . . We love him so dearly and we're so thankful for the man that he is."

KEY POINT SUMMARY

- It seems clear that how a leader treats those who follow is an imperative to success. When the leader treats those who follow with kindness, compassion, and integrity, the mission takes care of itself.
- The challenge for the transformational resilient leader is leading through crisis with an eye on future development. Winning in the moment, while important, is not everything. Sacrificing the future for the present is unacceptable to the

transformational leader. Leading with honesty and integrity is an investment in both the present and the future. It is your legacy.

- There are at least four "deadly sins" of moral leadership: (a) leading with a lack of candor, (b) accepting ownership of only those things that paint a positive picture, (c) failing to take responsibility, and (d) cheating.

- Acting with integrity is a process that culminates in employing these four questions to continually assess your own actions: Am I being deceptive? Does my action hurt anyone? Would I be comfortable if those I loved (e.g., partner, children) learned of my actions? Would I be hurt or angry if someone did this to me?

- Coach Mike Candrea, Olympic Champion and one of the greatest coaches in the history of college athletics, put people before winning. He said he works "backwards" having discovered he could never complete the mission unless he first took care of the people and led with integrity. Coach Candrea's career is perhaps best summarized by the words of Pericles, "What you leave behind is not what is engraved in stone monuments, but what is woven into the lives of others." The rest is history.

III

LEADING FROM STRENGTH

CHAPTER 10

SELF-CARE FOR PERFORMANCE

We couldn't write a book on leadership without including self-care. The human system requires healthy quantity and quality of sleep, balanced diet, adequate hydration, and physical exercise. These foundational pillars of wellness are necessary to withstand the demands of life, especially when challenging demands fall upon us. Although most leaders understand the connection between self-care and performance, "knowing" and "doing" are different things.

According to the Centers for Disease Control and Prevention (CDC; 2020), more than a third of Americans are not getting enough sleep on a regular basis. Researchers at the CDC and the American College of Sports Medicine also noted that Americans are more sedentary than they have ever been, as only 23% of the population regularly exercises (CDC, 2021b). And, in examining the prevalence of obesity in the United States from 1999 to 2018, the age-adjusted obesity increased from 30.5% to 42.4%, and the prevalence of severe obesity increased from 4.7% to 9.2% (CDC, 2021a).

For those of you looking to bolster your resilient crisis leadership skills, this chapter provides a brief overview to round out your knowledge and offer you specific takeaways to lift your self-care skills in order to optimize and sustain high performance over time. We review wellness as a foundation for performance and then take a deeper dive into unique considerations for performing under pressure. Indeed, it is this systematic approach that strengthens one's abilities when crisis strikes—performing under pressure requires one to optimize an already healthy system and to do so over time.

WELLNESS AS A FOUNDATION FOR PERFORMANCE AND RESILIENCE

One cannot perform if one is not well. As a leader, one must perform and in crisis, at high levels under pressure. Performance psychologist Jim Loehr developed a pyramid model of foundational elements needed for high performance in corporate industry. His Corporate Athlete model was created from the many lessons learned from athletic performers who have not only performed amazing physical and tactical feats under pressure but have sustained high performance efforts to legendary, Hall of Fame careers.

Loehr's performance pyramid highlights the foundation of one's physical capacity, which is associated with those actions that build endurance and promote mental and emotional recovery. Layering upon the physical capacity is one's emotional capacity, which Loehr and Schwartz (2001) identified as those actions that create an internal climate that drives the ideal performance state. Mental capacity, or the actions that focus the physical and emotional energy on the task at hand, is the third dynamic layer in the performance pyramid. Last, one's spiritual capacity, which is the peak of the pyramid, provides an individual with a powerful source of motivation, determination, and endurance necessary for high performance.

The physical elements provide the foundation to Loehr's performance model. Indeed, if a performer blows an ACL, you will see the performance limitations when they take to the court. The ability to jump, pivot, or laterally cut is compromised. No amount of mental fortitude will help them to overcome the physical deficit. While this example is one that clearly demonstrates the relationship between wellness and performance, other foundational elements of wellness may not initially be so apparent.

Wellness Foundations

Elite performers now not only focus on repair and rehabilitation of injuries but have evolved their training to incorporate crucial "unseen" elements of recovery. This form of "self-care" allows athletic and military Tier-1 performers to not only optimize performance but sustain the performance over time. The reason? There is a clear relationship between each wellness foundation (sleep, nutrition and hydration, and physical conditioning) and performance.

Sleep

The number one performance enhancer is sleep. That's right—not a pill or an injectable. Sleep. We know that sleeping at least 7 hours per night is recommended to maintain health and performance (Consensus Conference Panel, 2015). Research demonstrating that poor sleep health impairs performance is clear. Poor sleep health refers to insufficient sleep duration, poor sleep quality, fatigue and sleepiness, suboptimal sleep timing, irregular sleep schedule, and sleep/circadian disorders. These factors of sleep health impair one's performance in numerous ways. Specifically, poor sleep quality and quantity negatively impact muscular strength and speed, increase risk of injury and concussion, decrease reaction time and vigilance, reduce quality decision making and creativity, and impair learning and memory (Charest & Grandner, 2020).

International experts have offered several recommendations for optimizing sleep wellness for performance (Walsh et al., 2021).

201

First, adults need *at least* 7 hours of sleep per night. Remember, this is the *minimum* recommended. Elite performers likely require more to respond and recover from the physical, cognitive, emotional, and relational load of high performance: 7 to 9 hours of sleep is the suggested target.

Second, take power naps. Yes, research supports the positive effect of naps even for performers who get the suggested amount of nighttime sleep. Brief naps (ideally < 30 minutes, midday so as not to disrupt the sleep/wake cycles) can be beneficial in enhancing mood, alertness, and cognitive performance. Sleep replacement naps, or those for people who are not getting the recommended 7-hour minimum at night, can also help recovery. Sleep recovery naps are still suggested for midday and for no more than an hour. A significant key—if you take a nap and wake up feeling like you were hit by a truck, odds are you fell into deep sleep. Next time, reduce your nap time by 15 minutes and see if you feel more refreshed.

Finally, practice good sleep hygiene. Our habits influence many aspects of our wellness and performance, including our daytime alertness as well as the quantity and quality of our sleep. Consider implementing one of these sleep hygiene habits to improve your sleep:

- *Avoid stimulants (e.g., caffeine) in the afternoon and evening.* Remember the mean half-life of caffeine is approximately 5 hours. Half-life is the amount of time it takes for a substance to be reduced to half the original amount. So, despite drinking your quad shot Starbucks latte at 10 a.m., there is still a significant amount of the stimulant in your system by evening. If you double down and drink a cup of coffee in the evening, your system may struggle to wind down by 10 p.m. Given the long-term effects of caffeine, the American Academy of Sleep Medicine recommends that you don't consume it at least during the 6 hours before bedtime.

- *Be mindful of using alcohol or medications to fall asleep.* Drinking alcohol may help you fall asleep (or in higher doses, pass out). Yet, throughout the night, your body will be metabolizing the substance. Ever wake up around 3 or 4 a.m. after drinking too much the evening before? While alcohol itself is a depressant, the metabolites are stimulants. As a result, it can wreck the quality of your sleep with middle-of-the-night or early awakenings.

- *Engage in a wind-down routine with a sleep-conducive environment.* Sleep environments conducive to sleep are typically cool, dark, and quiet. Consider the texture of your pillow and bedding—invest in quality products that facilitate relaxation. Lastly, engage in a wind-down routine to help deactivate your system from the fast-paced day. Take time to develop routine practices that may include a warm bath, reading, listening to relaxing music, or doing a relaxation exercise such as deep breathing or meditation.

- *Practice stimulus control.* Our world is filled with engagement and stimuli. With the advancement of technology, we can engage socially or with work 24/7. Devices such as TVs, laptops, and mobile phones have generated access that improves our productivity and connection. Yet, if not careful, every strength becomes a weakness. Excessive screen time use before bed can result in us being more activated, not deactivated. Further, device use in bed then only trains our minds and bodies to consider the bed as a place of work, social media posting, or video calling. We recommend the bed remain a place for only sleep and sex. That's it. And, if you are unable to fall asleep or fall back asleep after middle-of-the-night awakening for 30 minutes, it is advised to get out of bed. Take some time to engage in a relaxing activity, and when you feel tired, return to bed and try again. Research has shown that the most powerful predictor of acute insomnia progressing to chronic insomnia is when people stay awake in bed over 30 minutes (Perlis et al., 2006). Their body becomes trained to be awake in bed, instead of asleep. So, wind down by turning off your devices, and if you have to send that one last email, get out of bed, stand by your nightstand, and hit send. Then, get back in bed for a solid night's sleep.

Just as hand washing will not treat your illness once sick, sleep hygiene will not treat a sleep disorder. If these sleep hygiene strategies are not helping, and you are still experiencing difficulties with nighttime sleep quality and/or daytime sleepiness, a referral to a sleep specialist is warranted. This is especially true if any of the following are causing problems for you in terms of your ability to function: (a) it takes more than 30 minutes to fall asleep or you are awake at least 30 minutes per night at least 3 nights per week, (b) you wake up frequently during the night for unknown reasons, (c) you have difficulty breathing during sleep or sometimes wake up gasping, or (d) you have problems staying awake during the day.

HYDRATION AND NUTRITION

Hydration and adequate fueling are foundational requirements for our bodies and systems to perform. Research on elite performers has illuminated the critical impact each has on our ability to perform. While you may not be a physical or tactical performer, resilient crisis leaders are still carrying a considerable cognitive, emotional, and relational load. For those in physically demanding environments, hydration and adequate fueling are even more significant.

Research indicates that deficits in water as little as 2% of body weight have shown to impede physical performance, and levels greater than this can lead to headache, sleepiness, impatience, and apathy (Institute of Medicine, 2005). Inadequate hydration impairs cognitive functioning required in a high performer such as a resilient crisis leader (Lindseth et al., 2013). The amount of water people need varies greatly depending on several individual factors such as physical size, sex, individual physiological requirements, workload, and the working environment. Water requirements also increase as a function of calories consumed. The larger the individual, the more calories/unit of time is expended, so more water is needed. Increases in ambient temperature as well as activity also increase the need for additional water.

To optimize hydration, it is recommended that people drink regularly throughout their workday and stop for short breaks every 2 to 3 hours. Individual hydration requirements vary considerably: recommendations of 11 to 16 cups for adults. It warrants mention that the American College of Sports Medicine (ACSM) noted that these recommendations may not be sufficient for highly active people who have higher fluid replacement needs (ACSM et al., 2007; Institute of Medicine, 2005). Finally, if you are not a fan of water, consider adding fruit so that it is more palatable, and find that go-to water bottle to help hydration become part of your day: Although, if these drinks are carbonated, they could lead to dehydration rather than hydration.

In addition to hydration, adequate nutrition is a foundational element of performance. Research has supported this finding when examining high performers in flight. In addition to poor communication between crew and unauthorized landings, pilot *hunger* has been associated as a critical factor in adverse outcomes. Researchers found that a missed meal alone was associated with a 22% increase in reported cognitive dysfunction (Bischoff & Barshi, 2003). In addition to these direct performance measures, a healthy diet has been linked to better moods, higher energy levels, and lower levels of depression—all of which increase productivity, creativity, and problem solving.

The brain is a blood-, glucose- and oxygen-hungry organ. As such, it requires certain foods that are proven to fuel your brain. Energy and macronutrient needs must be examined, especially carbohydrate and protein. These needs must be met during times of high activity to maintain body weight, replenish glycogen stores, and provide adequate protein to build and repair tissue. Fat intake offers essential fatty acids and fat-soluble vitamins as well as contributing calories for weight maintenance. Lastly, endocrine function can be affected by body weight and composition.

In sum, while individual hydration and nutritional needs may vary, the following suggestions can help to best fuel our systems for performance and resilience:

- Balanced nutrition. Consult with a qualified professional regarding shifts you can make in your diet to incorporate healthy carbohydrates, fats, and proteins that can best help you perform and bounce back in meeting the demands of crises.
- Hydrate for performance and recovery. Find that water bottle and integrate adequate hydration throughout your day. Considering adjusting your intake of other dehydrating agents, such as alcohol.

PHYSICAL ACTIVITY

A critical foundation of high performance and resilience, regardless of performance environment, is physical capacity. As mentioned earlier with the basketball player example, if we are physically compromised, our performance ability and ability to bounce back in adverse conditions are also compromised. From a wellness perspective, the health-promoting effects of exercise have been extensively documented going back centuries. Aerobic exercise, or that which increases one's heart rate and cardio strength and endurance, as well as anaerobic exercise, which tends to build strength and psychomotor skills, are both integral parts of exercise programs that boost performance and resilience.

Beyond the strength and skills that come from physical conditioning, research clearly indicates that the foundation of the ability to tolerate acute stress in crisis and to respond under pressure lies in physical conditioning. Research clearly indicates that one's ability to absorb the cognitive, emotional, and physical demands of crisis correlates to physical—specifically aerobic—conditioning. In addition to the performance gains from physical conditioning, consider the wellness benefits of a balanced exercise program:

- improve cardiopulmonary (heart and lung) efficiency
- boost learning and memory
- improve sugar metabolization
- reduce muscle tension
- lower resting blood pressure
- reduce body fat
- decrease in anxiety, depression
- improve self-esteem and interpersonal skills

In addition to these science-backed benefits of exercise and wellness and performance, research also supports the positive influence of exercise on leadership effectiveness. Leaders who exercise are rated significantly higher by their bosses, peers, and direct reports on their leadership effectiveness compared to those who do not exercise regularly. The time invested in regular exercise, even if it means spending less time at work, is correlated with higher ratings of leadership effectiveness (McDowell-Larson et al., 2002). So, consider finding a workout partner or blocking your schedule for a physical activity of your choice. Integrating exercise does not need to be time-consuming, as shorter, multiple periods of intensive exercise can be just as beneficial as longer, less intensive workouts. Find those 15-minute miniworkouts instead of trying to find a 2-hour block on the weekend.

Attitudes

Despite knowing that the aforementioned foundational elements help us perform under stressful demands, people still fail to include them in their daily lives because of a simple, yet powerful behavioral determinant—attitudes. Attitudes serve as a force multiplier, bringing to life the intersecting Wellness Foundations of sleep, hydration, nutrition, and physical exercise.

Let's consider our societal attitudes towards sleep, for example. We have all seen the bumper stickers or social media memes: "While you were sleeping, I was running!" How have the attitudes around sleep as an expenditure shaped our culture and, consequently, our behaviors? Sleep used to be considered a sign of laziness or wastefulness. Now, however, especially in Tier-1 performers in athletics and military, we have evolved in not only "knowing" that sleep is the number one performance enhancer, but we are also deliberately "doing" by prioritizing this recovery tool to maximize training gains and resilience. Advances in sleep training programs, such as Recovery Enhancement and Sleep Training (REST; Athey et al., 2017) as well as sleep technologies, have aided high performers to optimize sleep behaviors for their performance.

This shift did not happen by accident. Performance leadership observed the positive change from sleep optimization and its impact on performance outcomes as well as wellness outcomes such as injury mitigation and recovery. They now recognize the limitation of "more is always better" attitudes. Resilient crisis leaders are also now recognizing the same. The shift in understanding of sleep and self-care as an investment in our performance and resilience is being echoed by corporate leaders even amid crises. After enduring several months of the COVID-19 pandemic, John Donahoe (president and CEO of Nike) was asked at a leadership conference in July 2020 about how he stayed centered during this crisis. He shared the following:

> One of my greatest mentors, Tom Tierney, my predecessor at Bain, observed to me that every time in my career when I was stressed out, I worked harder by doubling down. One day he said to me, "Donahoe, when I come in and I'm either distracted or seem stressed or I'm irritable, do people notice?" I was like, "yeah, we notice." He then said, "Does that help you work more effectively? Or, when I come in and seem rested, calm, present, does that help you work more effectively?" "Yeah, I said." He shared back, "Then I would encourage you to take better care of yourself." I realized then that it was not selfish, but selfless, to take care of myself. It is important to be calm and present. I take care of myself now more. Mentally, emotionally, and spiritually. I'm getting more sleep. I need 8 hours of sleep. . . . I'm encouraging people to take care of yourselves. We aren't heroes. We have to support each other in taking care of each other. (Korn Ferry, 2020)

In sum, take time to reflect on your attitudes around self-care. If helpful, consider the shift that elite performers have made in reframing it as crucial recovery aiding our resilience and performance rather than thinking of self-care as a sign of being "soft." In a sense, for some, *not* taking the time for sleep and recovery is the lazy, easy way out. Making the deliberate effort to prioritize your sleep is hard work—although with the most considerable ROI.

Use Table 10.1 to check in with your performance foundation of self-care. Complete the self-assessment and then consider one

209

TABLE 10.1. Self-Care for Performance Check-In

Wellness domain	Action. Over the past month,	Never or seldom	Sometimes	Often	Almost always
Sleep	I prioritize my sleep by consistently getting at least 7 hours per night.				
Sleep	I feel rested or restored when I wake in the morning.				
Fueling	I eat regular meals and snacks to consistently fuel throughout the day.				
Fueling	I consistently take in water or other fluids to sustain my hydration needs throughout my day.				
Activity	I exercise moderately at least 30 minutes, three times per week.				
Activity	I find time each hour to stand or move.				
Attitude	I prioritize my wellness as a foundation for my performance.				
Attitude	I seek opportunities to care for myself and evolve my thinking to manage the demands I am facing.				

Note. Directions: For each action item, select the best answer.

aspect of recovery—sleep, hydration, nutrition, and exercise—that you could shift to help bolster your wellness for resilience and performance. With a newfound attitude that you are strengthening your ability to perform as a resilient crisis leader, the small habit shift can build over time and lead to a source of significant gains in weathering the impact of crises.

WHEN IT MATTERS MOST: PERFORMING UNDER PRESSURE

Transformative resilient crisis leaders engage in self-care to maintain a strong baseline from which to propel when crises strike. Performing under pressure *requires* this foundation as well as critical mental performance skills in order to meet the demands of dynamic and often ambiguous, uncertain circumstances and sustain performance under pressure over time. Elite performers rely on various mindsets to aid them in this response. Specifically, given their years of training and experience, many can draw upon this "muscle memory" and respond through a process of flow, or "letting it happen," and/or "making it happen" otherwise called "clutch" mindsets. The foundation of wellness for performance is critical as each of these mindsets require capacity in the brain's bandwidth to optimize functioning when performing under pressure.

Flow

Flow can occur at any point in performance and often is involved in the gradual accrual of confidence. People may experience flow in situations of uncertainty, situations of novelty, or experimenting/trying new things in performance (Csikszentmihalyi, 1997). The mental process of one experiencing flow can be described as (a) initial positive event, (b) receiving positive feedback, (c) experiencing an increase in confidence, (d) engaging in a challenge appraisal, and (e) having open goals or focusing on the process. Performers often experience intrinsic rewards (enjoyment, pride, satisfaction), intrinsic motivation, a sense of achievement, confidence about future performances, and an energizing effect from this mental state (Swann et al., 2017).

High performers may use an array of mental strategies or tools to engage a "flow" mindset. Analytical, critical thoughts, and excessive focus on the outcomes (e.g., winning/losing) can undermine this high-performance mindset. Given this, mental shifts toward positive distractions, which aid in focusing an athlete's attention *away* from the task at hand and enabling them to "switch off" the analytical, critical thoughts help to improve performance. Performance routines, breathing strategies, cues, and self-talk aid performers to center in this mindset. Fatigue, underrecovery, inadequate fueling/hydration, and a lack of physical conditioning compromise this mental process. Performers with cognitive bandwidth, strengthened with optimized self-care, can more effectively engage the mental tools to tap this flow experience.

Clutch

Clutch performance has been defined as one's ability to engage any superior performance that occurs under pressure demands (Otten, 2009). In a sense, clutch mindsets are about "making it happen" with a more intense and effortful state of heightened concentration and awareness. High performers engaging this mindset suddenly appraise the situational demands that are on the line or an outcome that is imminent. The process often is described as appraising the situation as a challenge, having fixed goals to execute, and the high performer decides to increase their intensity or effort (e.g., "flip a switch"). A high performer's subjective experience is often different than when engaging a flow mindset. Specifically, clutch is a state of complete and deliberate focus, intense effort, and heightened awareness, in which execution of specific skills is described as automatic rather than the whole state (as in flow). High performers are keenly aware and centered on the outcome focal point (e.g., finish line or outcome goal).

Underpinning the ability for one to tap this clutch mindset is one's capacity to experience stress, perceive the outcome of the situation as important, and succeed largely through effort (Hibbs, 2010). Performing under pressure taps all facets of performance—physical, emotional, mental, relational, and spiritual. If a resilient crisis leader does not do all that they can to bolster the performance system over time, optimizing when it matters most will be compromised.

PERFORMANCE SUSTAINMENT

Self-care also bolsters one's ability to be resilient and facilitate recovery to sustain performance over time. Certainly, it would be preferred if life only brought us one crisis at a time with timely recovery breaks in between. Unfortunately, this just isn't the case. Often resilient crisis leaders may be tackling a systemic crisis that produces smaller storms no different than tornados being spun off from a hurricane. The successive impacts and ability to respond over time can propel a resilient crisis leader to a legendary and systemic impact.

To sustain over time, one must mitigate the threats to an individual's resilience such as feeling overwhelmed, frustrated, and fatigued, as well as physical illness. Stressful events often lead to situations where demands are exceeding one's resources. While one can strategically cope by prioritizing tasks and consulting with others, it warrants mention that self-care or recovery strategies can also mitigate the impact of this emotional and relational load. Additionally, self-care bolsters one's brain energy to cope with emotional reactions such as frustration and effectively regulates arousal that leads to improved decision making. Fatigue can also be combatted to bolster resilience with adequate hours of quality sleep. Last, self-care strategies bolster resilience and the human system to fend off illness. Therefore, from these wellness and performance lessons, we must consider key strategies to lift our physical, emotional, mental, and spiritual capacity.

KEY POINT SUMMARY

- One cannot perform if not well. Transformative resilient leaders embrace self-care to bolster their ability to respond to the vast demands of crises and sustain optimal performance over time.
- Performance psychologist Jim Loehr emphasized key elements of high performance for the Corporate Athlete—physical, emotional, mental, spiritual—that enable them to optimize their performance and sustain it over time.
- Sleep is the top performance enhancer. It is recommended that an adult get at least 7 hours of sleep each night to support physical, mental, and emotional functioning.
- The foundation of ability to tolerate acute stress in crisis and to respond under pressure lies in physical conditioning; engaging in moderate physical exercise routinely is key.
- Hydration and balanced nutrition provide the necessary fuel to respond in acute crisis and sustain the response over time.
- Attitudes shape behavior. Consider your attitudes toward fundamental areas of wellness—sleep, nutrition, hydration, physical exercise.
- Optimally, leaders under pressure tap mental skills such as clutch and flow mindsets.

ACTION AGENDA AND QUICK REFERENCE CARD

1. **Focus on the mission and the people.** Every organization possesses two ongoing dynamic processes that are always engaged and operational: (a) mission-guided tasks and tactics, and (b) the psychological dynamics (people focus: morale, trust, interpersonal relationships). Transformative resilient leaders provide guidance for both processes. If you don't assume control, someone else will—often in stealth. You must constantly assess and implement the best balance of task and psychological support functions:

   a. Routine activities require an equal balance of mission and people foci.

   b. Crisis requires 80% to 90% focus on mission with 10% to 20% focus on people. As the crisis becomes chronic, shift more effort to people dynamics.

   c. In the acute aftermath of significant success, failure, or adversity, shift to 20% mission focus with 80% people focus.

   d. In situations wherein there are significant changes in policies and procedures, an equal balance on mission and people is required but in far higher intensities than in routine conditions.

2. **Continually earn your leadership position.** Transformative resilient leaders understand that leadership is derived from two sources: (a) assignment (assigned on the basis of seniority, education, or longevity) and (b) achievement (earned on the basis of one's mission-related actions). The transformative resilient leader acknowledges both and acts in a manner consistent with the latter to continually "earn" their leadership position. To do this, be visible and credible:
   a. Practice leadership by walking around.
   b. Reach out and connect formally and informally.
   c. Act in such a manner as to earn the followership of others.
3. **Listen before you speak.** Stress, fear, and anxiety all interfere with one's ability to follow even the most logical guidance. They cause people to revert to reflexive fear-based actions without consideration of the consequences. Transformative resilient leaders allow their followers to "vent" in a controlled environment to reduce stress. These leaders also understand that those closest to the work often understand the work processes better than anyone else. To listen more effectively:
   a. Give staff the opportunity to voice their personal and professional concerns in a safe environment.
   b. Ask open-ended questions, such as "What's your perspective?" and "What about this concerns you the most?"
   c. Validate feelings but redirect the conversation respectfully when necessary. Do not let the conversation spiral out of control.
   d. Pursue training in "psychological first aid" as recommended by *Scientific American* (Lewis, 2021a).
4. **Follow your own rules.** People trust actions, not words. Leaders must avoid the specter of hypocrisy. To demonstrate and model effective actions:

a. Practice the behaviors you prescribe; otherwise, you will be seen as a hypocrite.

b. Praise and thank them frequently.

c. Accept responsibility but share success.

d. Praise in public, critique in private.

e. Remember that whatever you say about another person will (eventually and always) be heard by that person.

f. Be consistent; otherwise, you will be accused of duplicity and thus deemed unreliable.

5. **Provide opportunities for connection.** Cohesive groups invariably handle stress and challenges better than non-cohesive groups, and they are better at strategic planning than noncohesive groups. To increase your group's sense of connectedness:

a. Schedule routine interactions, such as at the beginning or end of each shift.

b. Initiate impromptu interactions when critical incidents arise.

6. **Remember, there is no such thing as an information vacuum.** If leaders aren't communicating, others are usually the most distressed. To best provide information:

a. Provide information at scheduled intervals to all members of the team.

b. Provide information in advance of a change in practice or routine.

c. Provide information as soon as possible regarding a crisis or on-going incident.

d. When debriefing your group after an incident or change, discuss the following: What went well? What were the challenges, the worst parts? What did you learn? How can we apply our strengths to solve current problems?

7. **Communicate quickly and frequently during a crisis.** Fear and anxiety fuel chaos. Information is an antidote for anxiety and can empower people. Information generally comes in three variations: anticipatory guidance (what may happen), explanatory guidance (what happened and why it happened), and prescriptive guidance (recommendations or mandates for action). To best communicate relevant information during a crisis:

    a. Provide anticipatory guidance, explanatory guidance, and prescriptive recommendations whenever possible.

    b. Communicate quickly and frequently relevant to a critical incident or crisis.

    c. When commenting on specific incidents explain what happened, the cause, reactions (physical and psychological), what's being done to remedy the situation, and what can be done to prevent a similar incident in the future.

8. **Practice the 3 Ts of communication: transparency, timeliness, truthfulness.** Transparent, timely, and truthful communication is essential to create cohesion and maintain credibility. Cohesion fuels synergy, credibility predicts trust, and trust begins and ends with truth. Trust takes years to build, moments to destroy, and a lifetime to repair. Trust also predicts compliance. To practice the 3 Ts:

    a. Message frequently, anticipating questions and answering them in advance.

    b. Use repetition. Repeating an important idea 3 to 5 times maximizes retention while avoiding being pedantic or annoying. One good approach is to state an important idea once in the beginning of a communication, once in the middle, and once in the summary.

    c. Remember the primacy and recency effects: People remember what they hear first and what they hear last.

    d. If you don't know, say so, but hopefully also say so when you can provide the information.

    e. Stay current with social media regarding concerns, rumors, as well as shared experiences, positive and negative.

9. **When necessary, act decisively.** Transformation most readily arises from decisiveness because vacillation saps motivation and morale. Remember, the moment of absolute certainty may never arise. Inertia is challenging to overcome. To act decisively:

    a. Convey an optimistic vision and plan.

    b. Communicate.

    c. Be guided by your moral compass.

10. **Take care of yourself physically and psychologically.** Stress, fatigue, and burnout erode your effectiveness as a leader. They interfere with effective problem solving. They blind strategic vision, compromise tactical implementation, and increase errors by 35% to 75%. They get other people hurt. To take care of yourself:

    a. Get adequate sleep.

    b. Eat a balanced diet.

    c. Stay hydrated.

    d. Get physical exercise.

QUICK REFERENCE CARD: ACTION AGENDA FOR TRANSFORMATIVE RESILIENT LEADERSHIP

1. Focus on the mission and the people.
2. Continually earn your leadership position.
3. Listen before you speak.
4. Follow your own rules.
5. Provide opportunities for connection.
6. Remember, there is no such thing as an information vacuum.

7. Communicate quickly and frequently during a crisis.
8. Practice the 3 Ts of communication: transparency, timeliness, and truthfulness.
9. When necessary, act decisively.
10. Take care of yourself physically and psychologically.

SELF-ASSESSMENT TRACKING TOOL

Following is a summary table that you can use on a monthly basis to record your scores on the Five Pillars of Transformative Resilient Leadership.

TABLE B.I. Monthly Summary of Scores on Five Pillars

PILLARS	Jan	Feb	Mar	Apr	May	June	July	Aug	Sept	Oct	Nov	Dec
Vision												
Decisiveness												
Communication												
Support												
Integrity												

REFERENCES

American College of Sports Medicine, Sawka, M. N., Burke, L. M., Eichner, E. R., Maughan, R. J., Montain, S. J., & Stachenfeld, N. S. (2007). American College of Sports Medicine position stand: Exercise and fluid replacement. *Medicine & Science in Sports & Exercise, 39*(2), 377–390. https://doi.org/10.1249/mss.0b013e31802ca597

Ates, N. Y., Tarakci, M., Porck, J. P., van Knippenberg, D., & Groenen, P. (2019, February 18). Why visionary leadership fails. *Harvard Business Review*. https://hbr.org/2019/02/why-visionary-leadership-fails#

Athey, A., Alfonso-Miller, P., Killgore, W. D., & Grandner, M. A. (2017). Preliminary results of a sleep health intervention in student athletes: Perceived changes to sleep, performance, and mental and physical well-being. *Sleep, 40*(Suppl. 1), A450. https://doi.org/10.1093/sleepj/zsx050.1206

Avolio, B. J., Gardner, W. L., Walumbwa, F. O., Luthans, F., & May, D. R. (2004). Unlocking the mask: A look at the process by which authentic leaders impact follower attitudes and behaviors. *The Leadership Quarterly, 15*(6), 801–823. https://doi.org/10.1016/j.leaqua.2004.09.003

Bandura, A. (1982). Self-efficacy mechanism in human agency. *American Psychologist, 37*(2), 122–147. https://doi.org/10.1037/0003-066X.37.2.122

Bandura, A. (1997). *Self-efficacy: The exercise of control*. W. H. Freeman.

Baruchin, A. (2015). First aid for mental illness shows promise. *Scientific American Mind, 26*(2). https://www.scientificamerican.com/article/first-aid-for-mental-illness-shows-promise/

Bass, B. M. (1998). *Transformational leadership: Industrial, military, and educational impact*. Psychology Press.

Bass, B. M., & Riggio, R. E. (2005). *Transformational leadership* (2nd ed.). Psychology Press. https://doi.org/10.4324/9781410617095

Bennis, W., & Nanus, B. (1985). *Leaders: The strategies for taking charge*. HarperCollins.

Bischoff, J., & Barshi, I. (2003). Flying on empty: ASRS reports on the effects of hunger on pilot performance. In *One hundred years of flight: Proceedings of the 12th International Symposium on Aviation Psychology* (pp. 125–129). Wright State University, Dayton, OH, United States.

Bisson, J. I., Brayne, M., Ochbery, F. M., & Everly, G. S., Jr. (2007). Early psychological intervention following traumatic events. *The American Journal of Psychiatry, 164*(7), 1016–1019. https://doi.org/10.1176/ajp.2007.164.7.1016

Bloomberg News. (2021, November 23). *The winners and losers from a year of ranking COVID resilience*. https://www.bloomberg.com/news/features/2021-11-23/the-winners-and-losers-from-a-year-of-ranking-covid-resilience

Bonanno, G. A. (2004). Loss, trauma, and human resilience: Have we underestimated the human capacity to thrive after extremely aversive events? *American Psychologist, 59*(1), 20–28. https://doi.org/10.1037/0003-066X.59.1.20

Brosschot, J. F., Gerin, W., & Thayer, J. F. (2006). The perseverative cognition hypothesis: A review of worry, prolonged stress-related physiological activation, and health. *Journal of Psychosomatic Research, 60*(2), 113–124. https://doi.org/10.1016/j.jpsychores.2005.06.074

Buckner, R. L., Andrews-Hanna, J. R., & Schacter, D. L. (2008). The brain's default network: Anatomy, function, and relevance to disease. *Annals of the New York Academy of Sciences, 1124*(1), 1–38. https://doi.org/10.1196/annals.1440.011

Buford, M. A. (2019). *The servant way: Leadership principles from John A. Lejeune*. Bookbaby.

Burger, N. (Director). (2011). *Limitless* [Film]. Virgin/Rogue/Many Rivers Productions/Boy of the Year/Intermedia Film.

Burns, J. M. G. (1978). *Leadership*. Harper Collins.

Cannon, W. (1932) *The wisdom of the body*. W. W. Norton.

Carreyrou, J. (2015, October 16). How start-up Theranos has struggled with its blood-testing technology. *The Wall Street Journal*. https://www.wsj.com/articles/theranos-has-struggled-with-blood-tests-1444881901

Carroll, L. (1871). *Through the looking-glass, and what Alice found there.* McMillan.

Centers for Disease Control and Prevention. (2020, April 15). *Sleep and sleep disorders*. https://www.cdc.gov/sleep/index.html#

Centers for Disease Control and Prevention. (2021a, September 30). *Adult obesity facts*. https://www.cdc.gov/obesity/data/adult.html#

Centers for Disease Control and Prevention. (2021b, June 11). *Exercise or physical activity*. https://www.cdc.gov/nchs/fastats/exercise.htm

Charest, J., & Grandner, M. A. (2020). Sleep and athletic performance: Impacts on physical performance, mental performance, injury risk and recovery, and mental health. *Sleep Medicine Clinics, 15*(1), 41–57. https://doi.org/10.1016/j.jsmc.2019.11.005

Churchill, W. S. (1950). *The hinge of fate: The second world war* (Vol. 4). Houghton-Mifflin.

Consensus Conference Panel. (2015). Recommended amount of sleep for a healthy adult: A joint consensus statement of the American Academy of Sleep Medicine and Sleep Research Society. *Sleep, 38*(6), 843–844, https://doi.org/10.5665/sleep.4716

Coolidge, J. C., Jr. (1925, January 17). *The press under a free government* [Address before the American Society of Newspaper Editors, Washington, DC, United States]. https://archive.org/stream/foundationsofrep00unit/foundationsofrep00unit_djvu.txt

Coutu, D. L. (2002). How resilience works. *Harvard Business Review, 80*(5), 46–55.

Covey, S. R. (2004). *The 7 habits of highly effective people: Restoring the character ethic* (Rev. ed.). Free Press.

Csikszentmihalyi, M. (1997). *Finding flow: The psychology of engagement with everyday life.* Basic Books.

C-SPAN. (2000). *C-SPAN 2000 Survey of presidential leadership* [Data set]. National Cable Satellite Corporation. https://static.c-span.org/assets/documents/presidentSurvey/2000%20C-SPAN%20Presidential%20Survey%20Scores%20and%20Ranks%20FINAL.PDF

C-SPAN. (2009). *C-SPAN 2009 Survey of presidential leadership* [Data set]. National Cable Satellite Corporation. https://static.c-span.org/assets/

documents/presidentSurvey/2009%20C-SPAN%20Presidential%
20Survey%20Scores%20and%20Ranks%20FINAL.PDF

C-SPAN. (2017). *C-SPAN 2017 Survey of presidential leadership* [Data set].
National Cable Satellite Corporation. https://static.c-span.org/assets/
documents/presidentSurvey/2017%20C-SPAN%20Presidential%
20Survey%20Scores%20and%20Ranks%20FINAL.PDF

C-SPAN. (2021). *C-SPAN 2021 Survey of presidential leadership.* https://
static.c-span.org/assets/documents/presidentSurvey/2021-Survey-
Results-Overall.pdf

The Cut Staff. (2020, May 12). *9 ways to spot a frenemy.* The Cut/Vox
Media. https://www.thecut.com/article/how-to-spot-frenemies.html

Devilbiss, D. M., Jenison, R. L., & Berridge, C. W. (2012). Stress-induced
impairment of a working memory task: Role of spiking rate and spiking
history predicted discharge. *PLOS Computational Biology, 8*(9),
e1002681. https://doi.org/10.1371/journal.pcbi.1002681

Dickerson, J. (2020). *The hardest job in the world: The American presidency.*
Random House.

Dixon, D., Boland, R. J., Gaskin, J., Weeks, M. R., & Hunter, G. (2014).
In extremis leadership: Full mental jacket. *Academy of Management
Proceedings, 2014*(1), 11656. https://doi.org/10.5465/ambpp.2014.
11656abstract

Dixon, D. P., & Weeks, M. R. (2017). Leading in extremis situations: How
can leaders improve? In M. Holenweger, M. Jager, & F. Kernic (Eds.),
Leadership in extreme situations (pp. 251–275). Springer International.
https://doi.org/10.1007/978-3-319-55059-6_14

Donohoo, J. A. M. (2017). *Collective efficacy: How educators' beliefs impact
student learning.* Corwin/Sage.

Ehrmann, M. (1927). Desiderata [poem]. In M. Ehrmann (1948), *The
desiderata of happiness* (pp. 10–11). Crown Publishing Group.

Everly, G. S., Jr., & Athey, A. (2022). Crisis leadership (resilience) predicts
overall leadership effectiveness. *Crisis, Stress, and Human Resilience,
4*(1), 25–30.

Everly, G. S., Jr., Brelesky, G., & Everly, A. N. (2018). *Rodney makes a
friend.* RSI.

Everly, G. S., Jr., Everly, A. N., & Smith, K. J. (2020). Resilient leadership:
A partial replication and construct validation. *Crisis, Stress, and Human
Resilience, 2*(1), 4–9. https://www.crisisjournal.org/article/13322-
resilient-leadership-a-partial-replication-and-construct-validation

Everly, G. S., II, & Falcione, R. L. (1976). Perceived dimensions of job satisfaction for staff registered nurses. *Nursing Research*, 25(5), 346–347. https://doi.org/10.1097/00006199-197609000-00010

Everly, G. S., Jr., & Lating, J. M. (2019). *A clinical guide to the treatment of the human stress response* (4th ed.). Springer. https://doi.org/10.1007/978-1-4939-9098-6

Everly, G. S., Jr., & Lating, J. M. (2022). *The Johns Hopkins guide to psychological first aid* (2nd ed.). Johns Hopkins University Press.

Everly, G. S., Jr., Smith, K. J., & Lobo, R. (2013). Resilient leadership and the organizational culture of resilience: Construct validation. *International Journal of Emergency Mental Health and Human Resilience*, 15(2), 123–128. PMID: 24558699

Everly, G. S., Jr., Strouse, D. A., & McCormack, D. (2015). *Stronger: Develop the resilience you need to succeed*. AMACOM.

Farrer, M. (2020, October 7). New Zealand's COVID-19 response the best in the world, say global business leaders. *The Guardian*. https://www.theguardian.com/world/2020/oct/08/new-zealands-covid-19-response-the-best-in-the-world-say-global-business-leaders

Fiedler, F. E., & Garcia, J. E. (1987). *New approaches to effective leadership: Cognitive resources and organizational performance*. John Wiley & Sons.

Flannery, R. B., Jr. (1990). Social support and psychological trauma: A methodological review. *Journal of Traumatic Stress*, 3(4), 593–611. https://doi.org/10.1002/jts.2490030409

Fletcher, D., & Sarkar, M. (2012). A grounded theory of psychological resilience in Olympic champions. *Psychology of Sport and Exercise*, 13(5), 669–678. https://doi.org/10.1016/j.psychsport.2012.04.007

Forsyth, J. K., Bachman, P., Mathalon, D. H., Roach, B. J., & Asarnow, R. F. (2015). Augmenting NMDA receptor signaling boosts experience-dependent neuroplasticity in the adult human brain. *Proceedings of the National Academy of Sciences*, 112(50), 15331–15336. https://doi.org/10.1073/pnas.1509262112

Frederick, S. (2005). Cognitive reflection and decision making. *The Journal of Economic Perspectives*, 19(4), 25–42. https://doi.org/10.1257/089533005775196732

Galinsky, A. D., Maddux, W. W., Gilin, D., & White, J. B. (2008). Why it pays to get inside the head of your opponent: The differential effects of perspective taking and empathy in negotiations. *Psychological Science, 19*(4), 378–384. https://doi.org/10.1111/j.1467-9280.2008.02096.x

Gandhi, M. K. (1920). *The doctrine of the sword.* Young India.

Gardner, W. L., Avolio, B. J., Luthans, F., May, D. R., & Walumbwa, F. (2005). "Can you see the real me?" A self-based model of authentic leader and follower development. *The Leadership Quarterly, 16*(3), 343–372. https://doi.org/10.1016/j.leaqua.2005.03.003

Gellhorn, E. (1968). Central nervous system tuning and its implications for neuropsychiatry. *Journal of Nervous and Mental Disease, 147*(2), 148–162. https://doi.org/10.1097/00005053-196808000-00007

Gentile, M. C. (2010). *Giving voice to values: How to speak your mind when you know what's right.* Yale University Press.

George, B. (2003). *Authentic leadership: Rediscovering the secrets to creating lasting value.* Jossey-Bass/Wiley.

Gibson, L. (2006). Mirrored emotion. *University of Chicago Magazine, 98*(4). https://magazine.uchicago.edu/0604/features/emotion.shtml

Gladwell, M. (2000). *The tipping point: How little things can make a big difference.* Little, Brown.

Goodwin, D. K. (2005). *Team of rivals: The political genius of Abraham Lincoln.* Simon & Schuster.

Goodwin, D. K. (2018). *Leadership in turbulent times.* Simon & Schuster.

Gottman, J. M., & Levenson, R. W. (2002). A two-factor model for predicting when a couple will divorce: Exploratory analyses using 14-year longitudinal data. *Family Process, 41*(1), 83–96. https://doi.org/10.1111/j.1545-5300.2002.40102000083.x

Grantcharov, P. D., Boillat, T., Elkabany, S., Wac, K., & Rivas, H. (2019). Acute mental stress and surgical performance. *BJS Open, 3*(1), 119–125. https://doi.org/10.1002/bjs5.104

Gray, J. A. (1982). *The neuropsychology of anxiety: An enquiry into the functions of the septo-hippocampal system.* Clarenden Press/Oxford University Press.

Greenleaf, R. K. (1970). *The servant as leader.* Robert K. Greenleaf Center for Servant Leadership.

Greenleaf, R. K. (2002). *Servant leadership: A journey into the nature of legitimate power and greatness* (25th anniv. ed.). Paulist Press.

Harrison, E. F. (1993). Challenger: The anatomy of a flawed decision. *Technology in Society, 15*(2), 161–183. https://doi.org/10.1016/0160-791X(93)90001-5

Hattie, J. (2016, July 11–12). *Mindframes and maximizers: Visible Learning annual conference, 2016* [Conference proceedings]. National Harbor, MD.

Henry, J. P., & Stephens, P. (1977). *Stress, health, and the social environment: A sociobiologic approach to medicine.* Springer–Verlag.

Hibbs, D. (2010). A conceptual analysis of clutch performances in competitive sports. *Journal of the Philosophy of Sport, 37*(1), 47–59. https://doi.org/10.1080/00948705.2010.9714765

Hirdes, C., Grandner, M., & Athey, A. B. (2021). *C-SPAN presidential findings: The power of crisis leadership* [Unpublished manuscript].

Hebb, D. O. (1949). *The organization of behavior.* Wiley & Sons.

Hoffman, J. W., Benson, H., Arns, P. A., Stainbrook, G. L., Landsberg, G. L., Young, J. B., & Gill, A. (1982, January 8). Reduced sympathetic nervous system responsivity associated with the relaxation response. *Science, 215*(4529), 190–192. https://doi.org/10.1126/science.7031901

Homer. (2011). *The Iliad and The Odyssey* (S. Butler & S. Budin, Trans.). Canterbury Classics. (Original work published ca. 850–750 B.C.E.)

Institute of Medicine. (2005). *Dietary reference intakes for water, potassium, sodium, chloride, and sulfate* [Consensus study report]. The National Academies Press. https://doi.org/10.17226/10925

Institute of Medicine. (2013). *Ready and resilient workforce for the Department of Homeland Security* [Consensus study report]. The National Academies Press. https://doi.org/10.17226/18407

Inter-Agency Standing Committee. (2007). *IASC guidelines on mental health and psychosocial support in emergency settings.* IASC.

Ito, T. A., Larsen, J. T., Smith, N. K., & Cacioppo, J. T. (1998). Negative information weighs more heavily on the brain: The negativity bias in evaluative categorizations. *Journal of Personality and Social Psychology, 75*(4), 887–900. https://doi.org/10.1037/0022-3514.75.4.887

Jones, A. (2020, July 10). How did New Zealand become Covid-19 free? *BBC News.* https://www.bbc.com/news/world-asia-53274085

Jones, R. A. (1977). *Self-fulfilling prophecies: Social, psychological, and physiological effects of expectancies.* Lawrence Erlbaum Associates.

Kahneman, D. (2011). *Thinking fast and slow.* Farrar, Straus, and Giroux.

Kennedy, J. F. (1963, April 9). *Declaration of honorary citizen of the United States of America* [to Winston Churchill]. International Churchill Society. https://winstonchurchill.org/resources/speeches/1946-1963-elder-statesman/united-states-citizen/#

Kobasa, S. C. (1979). Stressful life events, personality, and health: An inquiry into hardiness. *Journal of Personality and Social Psychology, 37*(1), 1–11. https://doi.org/10.1037/0022-3514.37.1.1

Kolditz, T. A. (2007). *In extremis leadership: Leading as if your life depended on it.* Jossey-Bass/Wiley.

Konnikova, M. (2016, February 11). How people learn to become resilient. *The New Yorker.* https://www.newyorker.com/science/maria-konnikova/the-secret-formula-for-resilience

Korn Ferry. (2020, July 29). *Leadership in uncertainty* [Live webinar].

Kruger, J., & Dunning, D. (1999). Unskilled and unaware of it: How difficulties in recognizing one's own incompetence lead to inflated self-assessments. *Journal of Personality and Social Psychology, 77*(6), 1121–1134. https://doi.org/10.1037/0022-3514.77.6.1121

Krumboltz, J. D. (2009). The happenstance learning theory. *Journal of Career Assessment, 17*(2), 135–154. https://doi.org/10.1177/1069072708328861

Lakein, A. (1973). *How to get control of your time and your life.* New American Library.

Ledesma, J. (2014). Conceptual frameworks and research models on resilience in leadership. *SAGE Open, 4*(3). https://doi.org/10.1177/2158244014545464

Lejeune, John A. (1922, September 19). *Kindly and just* [Letter No. 1 to the officers of the Marine Corps]. Marine Corps University. https://www.usmcu.edu/Research/Marine-Corps-History-Division/Frequently-Requested-Topics/Historical-Documents-Orders-and-Speeches/Kindly-and-Just/

Lewis, T. (2021a, February 1). A step to ease the pandemic mental health crisis: A technique known as psychological first aid could help reduce COVID stress and anxiety. *Scientific American.* Retrieved June 26, 2021, from https://www.scientificamerican.com/article/a-step-to-ease-the-pandemic-mental-health-crisis/

Lewis, T. (2021b, March 11). How the U.S. pandemic response went wrong—and what went right—during a year of COVID. *Scientific American.*

Retrieved October 20, 2021, from https://www.scientificamerican. com/article/how-the-u-s-pandemic-response-went-wrong-and-what-went-right-during-a-year-of-covid/

Lincoln, A. (1905). *The Lincoln and Douglas debates in the senatorial campaign of Illinois* (S. A. Douglas & A. L. Bouton, Eds.). H. Holt & Company. https://lccn.loc.gov/14018156

Lindseth, P. D., Lindseth, G. N., Petros, T. V., Jensen, W. C., & Caspers, J. (2013). Effects of hydration on cognitive function of pilots, *Military Medicine, 178*(7), 792–798. https://doi.org/10.7205/MILMED-D-13-00013

Loehr, J., & Schwartz, T. (2001, January). The making of a corporate athlete. *Harvard Business Review.* https://hbr.org/2001/01/the-making-of-a-corporate-athlete

Lukianoff, G., & Haidt, J. (2018). *The coddling of the American mind: How good intentions and bad ideas are setting up a generation for failure.* Penguin.

Luthans, F., & Avolio, S. (2003). Authentic leadership development. In K. S. Cameron, S. E. Dutton, & R. E. Quinn (Eds.), *Positive organizational scholarship: Foundations of a new discipline* (pp. 241–271). Berrett-Koehler.

Machiavelli, N. (2006). *The prince.* (W. K. Marriott, Trans.). Waking Lion Press. (Original work published 1534)

Maguire, E. A., Frackowiak, R. S. J., & Frith, C. D. (1997). Recalling routes around London: Activation of the right hippocampus in taxi drivers. *Journal of Neuroscience, 17*(18), 7103–7110. https://doi.org/10.1523/JNEUROSCI.17-18-07103.1997

Marano, H. E. (2008). *A nation of wimps: The high cost of invasive parenting.* Broadway Books.

Maslow, A. (1943). A theory of human motivation. *Psychological Review, 50*(4), 370–396. https://doi.org/10.1037/h0054346

McClelland, D. C. (1961). *The achieving society.* Van Nostrand. https://doi.org/10.1037/14359-000

McDowell-Larsen, S., Kearney, L., & Campbell, D. (2002). Fitness and leadership: Is there a relationship? Regular exercise correlates with higher leadership ratings in senior-level executives. *Journal of Managerial Psychology, 17*(4), 316–324. https://doi.org/10.1108/02683940210428119

McGregor, D. (1960). *The human side of enterprise.* McGraw-Hill.

McLuhan, M. (1964). *Understanding media: The extensions of man.* Routledge.

Merton, R. K. (1936). The unanticipated consequences of purposive social action. *American Sociological Review, 1*(6), 894–904. https://doi.org/10.2307/2084615

Merton, R. K. (1948). The self-fulfilling prophecy. *The Antioch Review, 8*(2), 193–210. https://doi.org/10.2307/4609267

Mo, Z., Liu, M.T., & Wu, P. (2021). Shaping employee green behavior: A multilevel approach with Pygmalion effect. *Asia Pacific Journal of Marketing and Logistics, 34*(2). https://doi.org/10.1108/APJML-07-2020-0473

Moore, H. (2009). *A tender warrior: Leadership letters to America.* Simple Truths.

Nagy, G. (2013). *The ancient Greek hero in 24 hours.* Harvard University Press. https://doi.org/10.2307/j.ctvjghtrn

National Constitution Center Staff. (2021, October 8). *Franklin Pierce's murky legacy as president.* Interactive Constitution. https://constitutioncenter.org/interactive-constitution/blog/franklin-pierces-murky-legacy-as-president

The Navajo Nation. (2021, May 7). *Navajo nation now has over 100,000 fully vaccinated individuals* [Press release]. https://www.opvp.navajo-nsn.gov/Portals/0/Files/PRESS%20RELEASES/2021/May/FOR%20IMMEDIATE%20RELEASE%20-%20Navajo%20Nation%20now%20has%20over%20100,000%20fully%20vaccinated%20individuals.pdf

Naval Special Warfare Command. (n.d.). *SEAL ethos.* https://www.nsw.navy.mil/NSW/SEAL-Ethos/

Nietzsche, F. (1908). *Ecce homo* [Behold the man]. Insel-Verlag.

Nucifora, F., Jr., Langlieb, A., Siegal, E., Everly, G. S., Jr., & Kaminsky, M. J. (2007). Building resistance, resilience, and recovery in the wake of school and workplace violence. *Disaster Medicine and Public Health Preparedness, 1*(1), S33–S37. https://doi.org/10.1097/DMP.0b013e31814b98ae

Otten, M. (2009). Choking vs. clutch performance: A study of sport performance under pressure. *Journal of Sport and Exercise Psychology, 31*(5), 583–601. https://doi.org/10.1123/jsep.31.5.583

Ozer, E. J., Best, S. R., Lipsey, T. L., & Weiss, D. S. (2003). Predictors of posttraumatic stress disorder and symptoms in adults: A meta-analysis.

Psychological Bulletin, 129(1), 52–73. https://doi.org/10.1037/0033-2909.129.1.52

Parker, J. T. (2006). *Flicker to flame: Living with purpose, meaning, and happiness.* Morgan James Publishing.

Perlis, M. L., Jungquist, C., Smith, M. T., & Posner, D. (2006). *Cognitive behavioral treatment of insomnia: A session-by-session guide.* Springer.

Phillips, D. T. (1997). *Lincoln stories for leaders.* Summit Group.

Plumb, C. (2017, September 13). *Captain Charlie Plumb demo video: Pack your parachute* [Video]. YouTube. https://www.youtube.com/watch?v=c_ECWaz-CwY

Powder, J. (2021, August 5). *Keys to the Navajo Nation's COVID-19 vaccination success.* Johns Hopkins Bloomberg School of Public Health. https://publichealth.jhu.edu/2021/keys-to-the-navajo-nations-covid-19-vaccination-success

Robert, A. (2020). Lessons from New Zealand's COVID-19 outbreak response. *The Lancet. Public Health, 5*(11), E569–E570. https://doi.org/10.1016/S2468-2667(20)30237-1

Roosevelt, F. D. (1933). *First inaugural address.* The Avalon Project: Documents in Law, History and Diplomacy. https://avalon.law.yale.edu/20th_century/froos1.asp

Rosenthal, R., & Jacobsen, L. (1968). *Pygmalion in the classroom: Teacher expectation and pupils' intellectual development.* Holt, Rinehart & Wilson.

Rotter, J. B. (1966). Generalized expectancies for internal versus external control of reinforcement. *Psychological Monographs, 80*(1), 1–28. https://doi.org/10.1037/h0092976

Salpini, C. (2021, January 19). *What 6 charts say about the pandemic's impact on retail.* Retaildive. https://www.retaildive.com/news/what-6-charts-say-about-the-pandemics-impact-on-retail/593102/

Santayana, G. (2005) *Reason in common sense.* Project Gutenberg. (Original work published 1905). https://www.gutenberg.org/files/15000/15000-h/15000-h.htm

Scott, R. (Director). (2000). *Gladiator* [Film]. Dreamworks/Universal Pictures.

Seltzer, J., & Numerof, R. E. (1988). Supervisory leadership and subordinate burnout. *Academy of Management Journal, 31*(2), 439–446. https://doi.org/10.5465/256559

Shapiro, F. E. (Ed.). (2006). *The Yale book of quotations*. Yale University Press.

Sherden, W. A. (2011). *Best laid plans: The tyranny of unintended consequences and how to avoid them*. Praeger.

Shulman, G. L., Fiez, J. A., Corbetta, M., Buckner, R. L., Miezin, F. M., Raichle, M. E., & Petersen, S. E. (1997). Common blood flow changes across visual tasks: II. Decreases in cerebral cortex. *Journal of Cognitive Neuroscience, 9*(5), 648–663. https://doi.org/10.1162/jocn.1997.9.5.648

Smith, K. J., Emerson, D. J., Boster, C. R., & Everly, G. S., Jr. (2020). Resilience as a coping strategy for reducing auditor turnover intentions. *Accounting Research Journal, 33*(3), 483–498. https://doi.org/10.1108/ARJ-09-2019-0177

Smith, K. J., Emerson, D. J., & Everly, G. S., Jr. (2015, April 25). *Assessment of the roles of stress arousal, resilience, and burnout in the stress dynamic among auditors* [Paper presentation]. American Accounting Association Mid Atlantic Meeting, Philadelphia, PA, United States.

Smith, K. J., Emerson, D. J., & Schult, M. A. (2018). A demographic and psychometric assessment of the Connor Davidson Resilience Scale 10 with a US public accounting sample. *Journal of Accounting & Organizational Change, 14*(4), 513–534. https://doi.org/10.1108/JAOC-12-2016-0085

Smith, K. J., Everly, G. S., Jr., & Haight, G. T. (2012). SAS4: Validation of a four-item measure of worry and rumination. *Advances in Accounting Behavioral Research, 15*, 101–131. https://doi.org/10.1108/S1475-1488(2012)0000015009

Smith, R. S. (1995). Giving credit where credit is due: Dorothy Swaine Thomas and the "Thomas Theorem." *The American Sociologist, 26*(4), 9–28. https://doi.org/10.1007/BF02692352

Steinbeck, J. (1966). *American and Americans*. Viking Press.

Swann, C., Crust, L., Jackman, P., Vella, S. A., Allen, M. S., & Keegan, R. (2017). Psychological states underlying excellent performance in sport: Toward an integrated model of flow and clutch states. *Journal of Applied Sport Psychology, 29*(4), 375–401. https://doi.org/10.1080/10413200.2016.1272650

Tay, S. W., Ryan, P., & Ryan, C. A. (2016). Systems 1 and 2 thinking processes and cognitive reflection testing in medical students. *Canadian*

Medical Education Journal, 7(2), e97–e103. https://doi.org/10.36834/cmej.36777

Tedeschi, R. G., & Calhoun, L. G. (1995). *Trauma and transformation: Growing in the aftermath of suffering*. Sage. https://doi.org/10.4135/9781483326931

Tedeschi, R. G., & Calhoun, L. (2004). Posttraumatic growth: Conceptual foundations and empirical evidence. *Psychological Inquiry, 15*(1), 1–18. https://doi.org/10.1207/s15327965pli1501_01

Thomas, J. J. (2014). *The four stages of moral development for military leaders* [White paper]. The ADM James B. Stockdale Center for Ethical Leadership, U.S. Naval Academy. https://www.usna.edu/Ethics/_files/documents/Four%20Stages%20of%20Moral%20Development%20Thomas.pdf

Thomas, J. J. (2016, June 16). Leadership workshop [Presentation]. University of Arizona Softball Leaders Retreat. Tucson, AZ, United States.

Toffler, A. (1972). *The futurists*. Random House.

Tzu, S. (1983). *The art of war* (J. Clavell, Trans.). Delacorte. (Original work published ca. 500 B.C.E.)

United States. (1986). *Investigation of the Challenger accident: Report of the committee on science and technology*. House of Representatives, Ninety-ninth Congress, second session. Union Calendar No. 600. U.S. G.P.O. https://www.govinfo.gov/content/pkg/GPO-CRPT-99hrpt1016/pdf/GPO-CRPT-99hrpt1016.pdf

Vecchi, G. M., Van Hasselt, V. B., & Romano, S. J. (2005). Crisis (hostage) negotiation: Current strategies and issues in high-risk conflict resolution. *Aggression and Violent Behavior, 10*(5), 533–551. https://doi.org/10.1016/j.avb.2004.10.001

Verplanken, B., & Holland, R. W. (2002). Motivated decision making: Effects of activation and self-centrality of values on choices and behavior. *Journal of Personality and Social Psychology, 82*(3), 434–447. https://doi.org/10.1037/0022-3514.82.3.434

Vogelaar, A. L. W., van den Berg, C., & Kolditz, T. (2010). Leadership in the face of chaos and danger. In J. Soeters, P. C. van Fenema, & R. Beeres (Eds.), *Managing military organizations* (pp. 113–125). Routledge. https://doi.org/10.4324/9780203857106

von Clausewitz, C. (1984). *On war* (M. E. Howard, Trans.). Princeton University Press. (Original work published 1832)

Walsh, N. P., Halson, S. L., Sargent, C., Roach, G. D., Nédélec, M., Gupta, L., Leeder, J., Fullagar, H. H., Coutts, A. J., Edwards, B. J., Pullinger, S. A., Robertson, C. M., Burniston, J. G., Lastella, M., Le Meur, Y., Hausswirth, C., Bender, A. M., Grandner, M. A., & Samuels, C. H. (2021). Sleep and the athlete: Narrative review and 2021 expert consensus recommendations. *British Journal of Sports Medicine, 55*(7), 356–368. https://doi.org/10.1136/bjsports-2020-102025

Wallace, R. (Director). (2002). *We were soldiers* [Film]. Paramount Pictures.

Wanted a leader! (1861, April 25). *The New York Times*, 4. https://www.nytimes.com/1861/04/25/archives/wanted-a-leader.html

Werner, E. E. (2000). *Through the eyes of innocents: Children witness World War II*. Westview Press/Perseus.

Werner, E. E. (2005). Resilience and recovery: Findings from the Kauai longitudinal study. *Focal Point: Research, Policy, and Practice in Children's Mental Health, 19*(1), 11–14. https://www.pathwaysrtc.pdx.edu/pdf/fpS0504.pdf

Witte, K. (1992). Putting the fear back into fear appeals: The extended parallel process model. *Communication Monographs, 59*(4), 329–349. https://doi.org/10.1080/03637759209376276

Witte, K. (1994). Fear control and danger control: A test of the extended parallel process model. *Communication Monographs, 61*(2), 113–134. https://doi.org/10.1080/03637759409376328

Yukl, G. A. (2013). *Leadership in organizations*. Pearson.

Zak, P. J. (2017). *The trust factor: The science of creating high-performance companies*. AMACOM.

INDEX

237

ABOUT THE AUTHORS

George S. Everly, Jr., PhD, ABPP, FACLP, FAPA, is an award-winning author and researcher. His writings and research have helped shape the emerging field of disaster mental health. Over the course of 40 years, he has traveled to 39 countries on six continents to study firsthand crisis leadership and human resilience. Dr. Everly has held faculty appointments at the Johns Hopkins Bloomberg School of Public Health, the Johns Hopkins School of Medicine, Harvard University, and the Federal Emergency Management Agency. In addition, he served as an advisor to the Office of His Highness the Emir of Kuwait after the first Gulf War and later as an advisor to the New York Police Department in the wake of September 11, 2001. Dr. Everly is the author of over 20 books on stress, trauma, disaster, leadership, and human resilience. He was formerly chief psychologist and director of behavioral medicine at the Johns Hopkins Homewood Hospital.

Amy B. Athey, PsyD, CMPC, is a licensed psychologist and national leader in sport and performance psychology, crisis intervention, and developing nontraditional mental health and wellness programs for organizations. She currently serves on the Human Performance Team for the U.S. Naval Special Warfare Development Group. Dr. Athey has worked for more than 20 years providing clinical care, crisis intervention, and performance consultation for elite performers in sport, business, and the military. While chief wellness officer at the University of Arizona, she developed a peer-supported psychological first aid program in response to the mental health needs resulting from the COVID-19 pandemic. She has consulted for NCAA champions, professional athletes, Olympians, C-level executives, U.S. Special Forces, and the 2012 Rose Bowl Championship football team.

Dr. Athey earned a doctorate in clinical psychology from Loyola University in Maryland and has taught in university departments of kinesiology and psychology. She also received her bachelor of business administration degree from Roanoke College, where she was an All-American basketball player and inducted into the Roanoke College Athletics Hall of Fame.

Dr. Athey has published research and presented at international and national conferences as a leader in sport and performance psychology. She served as the inaugural PAC-12 Mental Health Task Force chair and drafted and motioned to the floor the first-ever NCAA Mental Health Legislation, which was unanimously approved. Dr. Athey also served on the NCAA Sleep and Wellness Task Force and the Executive Board of the American Psychological Association's Division 47 (Society for Sport, Exercise, and Performance Psychology).